THE

COMICON

AND

CONVENTION

SURVIVAL GUIDE

Cover Design by Craig W. Chenery
Illustrations by Crystalyn Reynolds & Angelina Reynolds

© 2015 Pop Culture Planet Publishing
All rights reserved
ISBN 13: 978-0-9909010-0-6
2nd Edition

A NOTE FROM THE AUTHOR

I love comicons and conventions and have attended events large and small across the country. I've seen the good, the bad, the ugly, the inspiring, the head scratching and the jaw dropping.

I have been extremely fortunate with my convention experiences. I have attended as a fan and had my fan boy moments meeting celebrities. I have attended as a costumer and posed for photographs with kids and adults alike. I have sat on team panels and talked about silly topics such as who would win in a fight between zombies and Stormtroopers. I've sat on serious panels discussing the future of the horror genre and mental illness. I've hosted my own panels and spoken for dozens of hours on topics near and dear to my heart. I've been in the audience asking questions to celebrities. I have had a vendor's booth and sold out of my books, I've had a vendor's booth and only sold one book. I've worked with moderators. I've been a guest author and signed books.

The convention world is my world where I feel at home and the attendees are my people. I bring you this book out of my love for the world of conventions. This book will guide you from the minute the tickets go on sale, to getting you home safely at the end of the event.

See you on the circuit!

Craig W. Chenery
August 2014

TABLE OF CONTENTS

CHAPTER ONE

INTRODUCTION

- **AN INTRODUCTION TO CONVENTIONS**
- **WHAT TO EXPECT AT A CONVENTION**
- **THE TYPES OF ATTENDEES**
- **ABOUT THIS BOOK**

*I*f you're reading this book, chances are you have been to, or are contemplating attending a comicon (or comic-con, depending on the event. Both versions are acceptable) or convention of some kind.

The Comicon and Convention Survival Guide is your insider's road map to help you navigate through the ins and outs of the convention world to ensure your experience is one you will long remember and hopefully entices you to come to a future event.

WELCOME TO THE WORLD OF CONVENTIONS

If you're new to the convention circuit or are experiencing

growth at a favorite event, they can become overwhelming very quickly. If not for the amount of people in attendance, then for the sheer number of options available to you over the course of the show. Conventions offer attendees a wealth of sights to take in and experience. There are likely to be dozens of guests for you to meet, hundreds of vendors to shop with, hundreds if not thousands of people in costume, panels on every subject under the sun and thousands of like-minded fans all congregating under one roof. *The Comicon and Convention Survival Guide* is your first class ticket into the world of conventions, whether it be at a small local genre-specific convention or a massive international comicon with A-list movie stars and sneak peeks at upcoming major Hollywood blockbuster movies.

Conventions are all about having a good time and making memories with friends and family. They are about immersing you in your hobbies and interests without being judged. With popularity booming at an exponential rate, it is safe to say that comicons and conventions are going to be here for a very long time. If you haven't gone to one yet, you don't know what you are missing out on.

THE GEEK SHALL INHERIT THE EARTH

Comicon. Just saying the name gets the blood pumping of fans from all over the world. Yet, there was once a time when announcing that you were heading to a convention for the weekend, when you would have been met with bursts of laughter, possible jeering or the scream of "nerd!" After all, comicons and conventions are for the diehard comic book fans and Trekkies, right? Fortunately, those days are gone.

In the last decade, something strange happened in the world of conventions. They became cool. Very, very cool.

You will now be hard pressed to find someone who either

has not gone to a convention or doesn't know someone who has. If you tell a friend or coworker that you are spending the upcoming weekend at a convention, chances are you will be met with comments like "aww, dude, I wish I was going". That is the great thing about conventions, everyone can go. There is no secret handshake or elvish password to memorize. You just buy a ticket and get your butt to the venue.

No longer tailored to just comic book artists, writers and the stereotypical cliché of basement-dwelling-mint-condition-action-figure-comic-book-collecting men who refuse to grow up (an inaccurate and unwarranted label, by the way) conventions across the globe have become massive mainstream pop culture events, bringing together fans from all kinds of cliques and areas of fandom into one united group.

YOU SAID THE 'M' WORD

Yes, I said mainstream. Let me explain.

While not all of the particular branches of fandom are popular or well known to much of the world, being able to go out and celebrate your love for an obscure franchise has never been more widely accepted than it is today. It is okay to be an ubergeek. It is now considered to be a character quirk to be able to speak Klingon. It is not a flaw that gets mocked. You can dress up as a superhero or Stormtrooper and not only will you not be ridiculed, people will be lining up to take their photograph with you. Children will hug you and tell you that you are their favorite character. You may even be asked to sign autographs.

There was a time when pop culture was written off as meaningless trash. It was considered mindless entertainment, with little to no social value. These days, it is doubtful you'll find someone in society who has not been affected by pop culture. Be it watching a superhero movie or a popular television show, reading a New York Times bestseller or quoting a famous phrase. Quotes like "May the Force be with you", "D'oh!' and "Beam me up, Scotty" have become ingrained in the social psyche.

We finally live in an era where our individuality is celebrated and not cause for humiliation or embarrassment. Superhero movies are earning record numbers at the book office and a quick look at the box office takings of the all-time top ten movies worldwide shows that seven of them are very successful pop culture franchises. Harry Potter, Transformers, DC and Marvel superheroes, James Bond and the Lord of the Rings. The top twenty includes Star Wars, Jurassic Park and Pirates of the Caribbean. The public loves geekdom and it has never been more apparent. Across the globe there are massive events where tens of thousands of like-minded people flock to share their franchise love. If you are a fan of pop culture, then chances are you will run into others with the same interests

Just in the U.S. alone, there are at least six annual conventions that are pulling in over 75,000 attendees. The largest of these being San Diego, which has reached 130,000. New York, Chicago, Phoenix, Salt Lake City and Seattle are quickly catching up. Then there are the smaller, more focused events that are geared towards specific genres or franchises. Attendance at these events ranges from a few hundred to a few thousand. Don't let the low attendance numbers scare you off. You can have just as much fun at a smaller, more intimate event as one of the larger ones.

WHERE DO I FIT IN?

Are you worried that the genre you support is too obscure and you won't fit in? Worry not! No matter your passion, you will find an event that tailors to your interests. While the big conventions cater to the broader market that encompasses many different genres, there are plenty of other smaller events that accommodate a more targeted audience. Keep in mind that due to the costs involved with putting a convention together, not all of the smaller events will necessarily be local to you. You may have to travel for some of the more genre or franchise specific events. For example, Los Angeles holds the annual Gallifrey One Doctor Who convention, which is one of only a handful of Doctor Who dedicated conventions in the United States at the time of printing.

Whatever your interests, if you keep your ear to the ground, you will find that someone somewhere is either planning a convention or has already held one. While there are many who claim that the internet has made us more antisocial, one of the most amazing things it has done for society is bring like-minded people together.

IS IT OKAY TO GEEK OUT IN PUBLIC?

Comicons and conventions are very liberating. They allow you to throw your inhibitions aside and let you geek card hang out for all to see and you can do it with pride. Do you want to dress up as a Starfleet Officer from Star Trek? No problem. Do you want to be Willrow Hood, the way, way, way in the background "Ice Cream Man" character from The Empire Strikes Back? Knock yourself out. Do you want to be a Chobit? No, not one of the pointy eared fellows from J.RR Tolkien's epic Middle Earth saga. The pointy eared little computers from the Japanese manga and anime. The point is, you can wear your geek heart on your sleeve and you won't be judged or outcast. Conventions are a time to celebrate your inner geek.

Sure, they still allow fans of mint-on-card action figures

to add to their collections, or if you're like me, a "let's rip the damn thing open and display it" type collector. If you collect autographs, you can meet celebrities, you can buy comic books or speak Huttese and no one will judge or criticize. The nerdy minutia that fans love so much becomes the social norm. Knowing the components of the various wands in Harry Potter doesn't make you an outcast, the knowledge becomes currency and it is traded for other similar nuggets of information. You can meet other Hogwarts historians and trade wand specs for spells and compare your research on the Black family tree. Your ten feet long Tom Baker scarf isn't a prop to be laughed at; it just shows that you never forgot your first doctor.

WHAT TO EXPECT AT A CONVENTION

Due to individual tastes and interests, everyone takes away something a little different from an event. Not all attendees are there to visit the celebrities or see sneak peeks of upcoming movies. Some are fans of obscure comic book artists, while some are looking to pick up a particular piece of artwork or collectible. Some simply come to see or be seen. Your experience will be part of your own unique adventure.

While no two conventions are held the same way, you can expect to find a healthy combination of the following features available to attendees.

- Celebrity guests of varying fame and popularity
- Vendor area
- Exclusive merchandise
- Artist and author areas
- Trivia events
- Fan panels
- Exclusive film footage and film festivals
- Costume competitions and balls

• Fashion shows

Although you will most likely not be able to do everything you want to do over the course of the event, you will have a day or weekend crammed full of things to do and you will leave feeling satisfied.

SHOULD I STAY OR SHOULD I GO?

If your local town or city is holding a convention, by all means go. Don't just wait around for the bigger out-of-state events. Smaller local events with the right support can grow into a big convention in a relatively short amount of time. No convention held its inaugural event to 100,000 attendees. They all had to start somewhere. For example, Phoenix Comicon started in 2002 and opened to 357 attendees running for half a day. By 2014, it had become a four day event hosting over 77,000 people all through the support of the local fan base and loyal attendees. San Diego Comicon has capped at 130,000 the last few years, but it certainly did not debut to numbers anywhere near close to that.

Some of the smaller events are also a great way of having a few more minutes with a celebrity guest that you may not get at a larger event where thousands of people are clamoring for the same autograph. I was recently at a horror event in Phoenix and had the privilege of meeting an author I had admired since I was a child. As this was a smaller event, I was able to spend fifteen minutes chatting with him about his work and the influence it has had on me. At a larger convention, this may not have been possible. Try not to write off smaller conventions just because they don't have the big name celebrities. Besides, you never know when you'll meet an artist or author who is one book away from international fame and stardom. Everyone has to start somewhere.

Conventions are also extremely good for the local economy. Cities are embracing these events as they are considerable revenue earners for the municipalities that host them. Local hotels completely sell out and restaurants have lines of customers wrapped around the building. Vendors are able to expand their markets and artists and authors find themselves with a new audience. Not to mention the considerable amounts of sales tax the events generate for the cities and state. In short, everybody wins.

WHAT IS IN THIS BOOK?

While you can of course simply just show up to a convention, you can have more fun if you take a little time to prepare before going. There is a level or preparedness you can undertake to ensure you and the people around you have a great time. As conventions continue to grow in size and popularity, it will become even more important for attendees to be familiar with convention etiquette.

This guide is an in depth look at the world of conventions and the best way to navigate the ever growing landscape. It is broken down into three main sections, including before the event, during the event and after the event. These sections address attending, shopping, photography, costumes, guests, panels and more. The majority of attendees will fall into at least one of these categories. There are also chapters on con etiquette, safety and harassment.

I am very fortunate to have been able to experience all sides of the convention world. I have appeared as a guest author, I have sat on panels, I have attended panels, I have gone in costume and I have gone as a fan boy and geeked out for the entire weekend spending as much disposable income as humanly possible. Each way is different from the other and it is hard to pick a favorite, as all have their pros and cons. Going as a guest is fun as you get to meet your audience

and fans. However, you have to keep your game face on all day. No one wants to meet a grumpy guest. While this is very rewarding, the days can be extremely long. Attending as a fan allows you to be in geek mode all weekend long and meet your favorite guests and celebrities, but you'll be spending a good portion of you time waiting in line. We'll get to that a bit later.

No matter how you attend an event, *The Comicon and Convention Survival Guide* will point you in the right direction to ensure you enjoy your experience.

WHAT THIS BOOK IS NOT

This book is designed to help you get the most out of your event. It is not an inside guide to help you circumvent the system or become a master of cheating the rules. While I would love to tell you that there is some industry secret to help you cut to the front of every line, or some secret handshake that will allow you to meet every celebrity free of charge, there isn't. There is no hidden password to help and obtain every convention exclusive. All attendees must adhere to the same set of rules. Think of it as going to a buffet. There is a lot of great food to choose from, but unfortunately you can't eat everything. Conventions are set up the same way. It is not possible to do everything, unless you master the art of cloning. Pick and choose what you want to do and use *The Comicon and Convention Survival Guide* to help ensure your experience is an enjoyable one.

Conventions are organized so that if everyone sticks to the rules, everyone can have fun. A lot of work goes into the planning and operation of these events. The systems aren't designed to be cheated. You may not like having to stand in line to get an autograph, but the person in line behind you is going through the same thing. Relax, have fun and a convention can be a wonderful experience.

PART 1
BEFORE THE EVENT

CHAPTER TWO

PRE-EVENT PLANNING

- **PURCHASING TICKETS**
- **TRAVELING**
- **WEAPONS RULES AND POLICIES**
- **GENERAL EVENT RULES AND ETIQUETTE**

*T*he weeks and months leading up to a convention can be long and arduous as you sit watching the time pass by. You're naturally going to be excited for the event, but instead of clock-watching and counting down the days, use your time to get some of your ducks in a row before it arrives. Some pre-event planning can save you time, money and potential heartache if you wait until last minute to buy tickets or look for a hotel room.

TICKETS

Before you can even think about attending a convention, the first thing you are going to need is a ticket to get in the door. Not every event uses paper tickets. Some use badges, lanyards or wristbands to identify guests.

Most conventions will allow you to buy your tickets online through their website. Some may also use a third party ticketing or social website. You will need to decide how long you are going to be at the event. If it is a three day event, are you planning on going for all three days or just Saturday? If you plan to just go on Friday and Sunday, it may be cheaper to buy the full event ticket instead of just the multiple single day tickets. Consider all of the options before just jumping in, as there may be an offer that is more cost effective. The less you spend on a ticket, the more money you will have to spend at the event.

If a particular guest you want to meet is at the event for all three days and you only plan to go for one day, try and go on Friday if your schedule permits. It is typically the slower of the three days, with many people still at work. Saturday is generally the busiest day, with Sunday not far behind. If you go during a quieter time, you may also be able to spend a little more time chatting with the guests.

The Early Bird Catches the Discount

Most conventions reward fans who buy tickets early with significant discounts. In some cases the savings can be as much as 50% or more. Generally, many of the bigger guests have not been announced when tickets first go on sale and event organizers count on attendee's goodwill to buy tickets in advance. If you have been to the convention before or have followed previous guests, you can determine if buying the early bird pass is beneficial. Many of the bigger events will hold off on naming popular guests until closer to the event date. As the date of the event approaches, prices will go up, eventually reaching full price.

Try to avoid buying tickets at the door if you can. Not only will it cost more, but it can seriously delay you getting inside the venue. Pre-ordering doesn't just allow you to save money; it makes picking up the badges at the registration booth much faster, allowing you more time on the convention floor. Many conventions also allow you to pick up your badges or tickets from a separate check-in area before the doors open.

To save time, some of the smaller events offer the option of printing your tickets at home.

Third Party Tickets

If you are willing to risk the event selling out, in the weeks leading up to the convention, discount websites such as Groupon and Living Social may offer significantly discounted tickets to certain events. Although, not every event will use these sites, some do and if you're lucky, you can find some good deals. I recently picked up two single day tickets to a local horror event that should have cost $75, but I got them for the screaming deal of $17.

No Refunds

Make sure you are happy with your purchase and can definitely attend the event before you buy the tickets. Almost all sales are non-refundable. Some are also non-transferable, although that is harder to enforce with general entrance tickets with no name on them.

Avoid Scalpers

As with any event, be cautious of buying tickets on the secondary market. Open market sites like Craigslist and Backpage are rampant with people selling counterfeit tickets to all kinds of events. Handing over $200 for ten tickets to San Diego Comicon in a Circle K parking lot fifty miles from your house is not going to end well. At least not for you. Very few people are going to sell a $300 weekend ticket for $20. Unless of course, it is fake or stolen. Check with the conventions policies on reselling tickets and if in doubt, side with caution. Your wallet will thank you in the long run.

Delays Can Be Costly

All conventions large and small have the potential of selling out. Fire code standards will only allow for a certain number of people to be in a building at any given time and convention organizers must adhere to these rules. So don't wait until last minute to buy tickets unless it is absolutely necessary. If you do wait until the final days leading up to the event, be prepared for disappointment. With the popularity of conventions growing, more and more events are selling out.

Media Passes

Most conventions have a limited number of media passes available for attendees who are part of the media and wish to report on the convention. If you run a podcast from your basement that averages two listeners a month, don't apply for a media badge. You're not a member of the media. You may have good intentions and high hopes, but without an audience, you are a fan like everyone else. Focus on building up your audience so you have people to report your findings to. Then apply for a media pass.

TRAVELLING

Regardless of whether a convention is in your city or half way across the country, you will need to factor travelling into the equation. There are numerous options available to get you to the event. Also, take into consideration how you will get around town after the venue closes for the day.

TRANSPORTATION

Unless the event is on your front door step, you will need to determine how you are going to get yourself to the venue.

Driving

The obvious option is hopping in your car and driving. This idea is all well and good, but if the event is expecting a large number of attendees, you could find yourself fighting for a parking space with 40,000 other cars and parking becomes a nightmare.

Parking

If driving is your only option, check out a city map and determine where the parking lots are in the area. If you are planning on buying a lot of merchandise, try to park at the end nearest to the vendor hall. There is nothing worse than buying an armful of merchandise only having to walk over a mile to get back to your car. While your options may be limited, using a tool like Google Earth can get you familiar with the area relatively quickly. Then you can determine if there are smaller, out of the way lots that may be worth looking into.

Be warned that parking fees can add up very quickly especially if you need to go home for a costume change. Most parking lots charge anywhere from $10 - $20 a car with no in and out privileges. Over the course of the weekend, parking can get very expensive; consider using a nearby hotel as an alternate option.

Alternate Transportation

Many cities have efficient bus or light rail systems. Determine if you are better off parking away from the venue where parking is probably much cheaper, if not completely free and using mass transit to get to the event.

The added bonus of using public transportation is the odd looks you get from other passengers if you are in costume.

Shuttles

Some hotels may offer periodic shuttles to the event. This is not a guarantee, so check with the hotel prior to booking to see if this is a service they provide.

Taxi Cabs

While taxis are always an option, be mindful that they can get very expensive if driving more than a mile or two.

DOUBLE YOUR LUGGAGE

If you are coming in from out of state, chances are you took a flight in. If you own nesting suitcases, pack your suitcase in the next size above it. If you are checking in your bags, you are already paying the check-in fees. This allows you to get a second suitcase to the event for free so you can pack up any extra items you may buy during your adventure. You'll have to pay the baggage fee on the return flight, but it will save you money on the trip out. Many hotels and convention centers have shipping areas where you can ship items back home, but it isn't cheap. As with many other features, you are paying for the convenience.

HOTELS

If you are at an out-of-state event, chances are you will have booked a hotel room. However, even if the event is local, there are still benefits to renting a room and having it close by. A nearby staging area is an ideal location to store costumes and supplies and can be a real life saver. Most larger conventions will negotiate discounted rooms with nearby hotels and many hotels also serve as overflow venues, hosting after hours parties and events that the main venue may not be able to cater to. As many conventions are held in hotel ballrooms and conference rooms, staying in the same hotel can be extremely useful.

You Snooze You Lose

If you are going to rent a hotel room, don't put it off until the last minute. The rooms, especially those with a discounted event rate, sell out very quickly and you can soon find yourself having to get a hotel many miles away from the venue, which will incur more transportation costs.

Shower, Shower, Shower

This may seem pretty obvious to most people, but you have a shower in your hotel room, use it! Clean is good. Clean is very good and very much appreciated by anyone who comes into contact with you.

It is almost inevitable that at some point during the event you will stand behind, next to, or in front of someone who smells a little ripe. Don't be that person. Your neighbors will love you for it.

This rule applies even if you don't have a hotel room and are coming straight from your house. Shower, shower, shower. It is what separates us from the dark ages. That and smart phones.

Stock Your Room

Walking around for hours on end burns a lot of calories and while snacks are available in the venue, you will pay for the convenience. Be sure to bring a few of your own and keep extras in your room. I haven't been to a convention yet that has forced me to surrender a hidden Twix at the front door. The same goes for the hotel, don't buy snacks from the lobby. Find a store in the area to stock up on drinks and snacks. They will be considerably cheaper and puts more money in your pocket to spend. If your hotel room does not have a refrigerator, buy a cheap Styrofoam disposable cooler to keep your snacks and drinks cold.

Hotel Etiquette

Remember, when hanging around in the hotel that there may be guests staying there who are not part of the convention. Don't hang around in corridors or elevators blocking access to amenities. Hotel guests need to be able to use the facilities too.

Behave respectfully and in a manner that benefits the convention at all times while in the hotel. The rules of the convention extend to the hotel, especially if the hotel is hosting additional programming. If you are caught being disruptive, you may have your badge revoked. Be on your best behavior at all times. You are a representative of the event. Don't make the hotel regret allowing convention attendees to use their facilities.

THE VENUE

Conducting a little research on the venue before you arrive at the event can help you save time from wandering around like a lost puppy. Not being familiar with the lay of the land is a good way to lose out on any event exclusives you were hoping to pick up or miss a celebrity panel you wanted to attend. Knowing where a specific vendor or room is located, means you can head straight over there as soon as the doors open.

Venue Maps

The majority of convention centers have online maps that you can view or download. These will allow you to determine how the space is set up. You can see where the vendors are that you want to visit, the celebrities you want to meet and the conference rooms for the various panels are located. Not all conventions have sufficient signs posted and it is easy to get turned around or lost. It won't be painless, as there are often unavoidable last minute changes, but it will make the experience go a bit smoother.

Amenities

The venue website should give an overview of the available amenities on site, such as ATM machines, food options and bathrooms.

Try to Avoid On-site ATM's

There will most likely be an ATM on the premises. Don't be fooled by this happy looking machine, eager to spit $20's out at you so you can have a good time. These machines will charge convenience fees that range from anywhere between $2 and $5. As these are generally privately owned and not affiliated with a bank, your bank will most likely charge an additional "convenience" fee on top of that also ranging between $2 and $5. Withdrawing $20 could ultimately end up costing you $10 in service fees.

Plan accordingly and pull as much as you think you will need for either the rest of the day or the rest of the event. Pulling $20 five times, could end up costing you anywhere from $20 to $50. Pulling $200 could cost up to a hundred dollars. It is easy to write off a few dollars at first, but it can add up really fast and before you know it, half of your budget for the weekend has been wasted on needless fees.

THE EVENT

Although the event may be weeks or months away, there are many ways you can keep up to date on news and changes to the convention.

Online

Most conventions will have a central and official website that will keep you up to date on the event. Consider this your primary resource for all official notices. You will find guest announcements and cancellations, autograph schedules, details on event exclusives and room assignments for panels.

There's An App for That

Many events have their own Android and iPhone apps available for download. These applications offer tools related to the event including alerts and calendars. Try to install the app before getting to the venue as coverage can sometimes be spotty.

Follow Social Media

Social media can be a great asset in planning your event. If you don't have access to an app, see if the convention has a Facebook or Twitter account. Most will post updates real time throughout the event notifying attendees of room changes, guest cancellations and any other unexpected schedule changes.

PLAN AHEAD

With a seemingly overwhelming amount of programming available, you can save you a considerable amount of time by making a rough plan of what you want to do. That way you are not wasting time just walking around aimlessly, unsure of where you are heading.

Schedules

Prior to the start of the event, the organizers should have posted a calendar of events on their website. Take some time to read through it so that you can see which events you want to do and the times you will need to be in a particular location. These schedules are generally available at the convention, but that may not always be the case depending on the organizers and the budget available for printing.

GUESTS

One of the major selling points of any event is the guest list. The popularity of guests generally depends on the size of the event and the budget available to bring the guests out. Not every convention can afford to have A-list Hollywood celebrities.

Guest Announcements

For many attendees, waiting for the guest announcements is one of the most exciting parts of the pre-event activities. Will they announce someone you don't know or someone you have been a fan of all your life? Maybe it is someone you didn't even know you were excited to meet. It is a great feeling hearing a guest announced that you have idolized for thirty years.

Don't Be a Jerk

Most events will provide updates on their various websites on the status of new guests. If you are not a fan of a particular guest, refrain from posting comments like "who cares?", "boring" or "oh, man, I can't stand this person". Just because you do not approve of a particular guest, that does not mean that there aren't others who are excited about the announcement. These kinds of comments take what is supposed to be a happy announcement and make it negative.

I follow numerous conventions on Facebook and almost without fail, every time a new guest is announced; someone feels the need to chime in with their negative opinion. This may sound harsh, but nobody cares whether you like the guest or not and people's opinions will not be swayed because you aren't impressed. In fact, it only makes you look like a tool. Not every guest is going to be an A-list Hollywood movie star. No convention on the planet, not even San Diego Comicon, is made up of all A-list guests. It would be incredibly expensive and the lines would be a nightmare. Guests of all levels of fame and popularity make for a well-balanced event. Getting bent out of shape because they announced a comic book guest instead of Robert Downey Jr. just doesn't make sense.

Guest Cancellations

Guest cancellations are an unfortunate element of conventions, but it is one that is unavoidable and affects conventions large and small. At some point, one or more scheduled guest on the roster is likely to cancel. This could be someone you are not interested in meeting, or it could be the sole reason you are going. It is almost inevitable that this happens.

It is written into the contracts guests enter into with the event that their appearance is contingent on them not working. As guests can schedule events many months in advance, changes may happen to their schedule that are out of their control. Remember, they are first and foremost actors, musicians, artists and authors. They have to produce work to make a living.

Seriously, Don't Be a Jerk

These cancelations affect everyone. Event organizers don't enjoy announcing guest cancelations and guests don't enjoy canceling. Taking to social media to denounce the event and its organizers doesn't change anything and screaming fixes nothing. Throwing a cyber-tantrum will not make the celebrity suddenly change their mind. If this particular celebrity is your sole reason for going, you are taking a risk if you are attending an event for only one person. Try to find multiple reasons to attend a convention to avoid potential disappointment.

SOCIAL WEBSITES

Conventions are even more fun if you go with a group. Not only can you share in your fandom, but people can hold your place in line if you have to go to the bathroom or you can split up and get exclusives for each other.

If your friends aren't in to it, websites like Meetup.com can connect you with social groups with similar interests.

WEAPONS

Venues understand that weapons may be a part of your costume, but there are strict rules to adhere to regardless of the event. Be sure to check with the weapons policy before bringing a weapon to an event. If you show up with a banned weapon you will be asked to take it off of the premises, don't get snooty with the security guards, they are just doing their job. Different states, cities and venues have different rules. Be sure you know them before going to the event. Ignorance is not an excuse. Trust me, you don't want to stand for an hour to get in, only to have to go back to your car, drop off your weapon and comeback to the venue. You know that exclusive item you wanted to get? Yeah? Well, it is probably long gone by now.

Prop weapons are generally allowed as long as they are composed of cardboard, foam, wood or other soft or light materials and are in no way dangerous to fellow attendees. Prop firearms are allowed only if they cannot be mistaken for real weapons.

Many cities require the barrel of prop firearms to be covered with brightly-colored caps or the weapon needs to be peace bonded by a law enforcement or security officer at the event.

Peace Bonding

Peace bonding is the process of labeling a weapon so that it is suitable for use at a convention. The review is generally done by an off-duty law enforcement officer or on-site security on a case by case basis. If a costume weapon is reviewed and security determines it to appear dangerous, it shall be peace bonded before being allowed into the venue.

Peace bonded weapons will usually have a bright orange or yellow tag attached to a non-intrusive area of the prop weapon. The tag must remain visible at all times. If your tag is not visible, you will be stopped by event security.

For bladed weapons, such as a sword, the peace bond process will secure the weapon inside the sheath. At no time shall the weapon be removed from the sheath while attending the event. Removal will likely result in expulsion from the event.

In the event a weapon is not allowed it the venue, i.e. if it cannot be peace bonded, you will either have to return the weapon to your vehicle or hotel room or it will be confiscated. If a costume weapon is confiscated it will be tagged with the owners name written on the tag. Confiscated weapons will only be returned to the owner when they are leaving the event. Most venues are exempt of responsibility for any damage to confiscated weapons. You have been warned.

Bows can be allowed, providing all arrows have soft tips.

If you win or purchase a weapon from a vendor, you will still need to be familiar with the weapons policy and prepared to remove it from the venue if you are unable to have it peace bonded. Hopefully you parked somewhere close.

Projectile Weapons

Projectile weapons are firearms that are designed to fire a projectile, i.e. pellet guns, BB guns, air guns, paint ball guns, dart guns, Nerf guns, water guns, rubber band guns, potato guns, crossbows and any other kind of ammunition. These are not permitted into conventions with ammunition.

Generally, blunt wooden staves, knives, swords, and bullwhips are permitted. They must be sufficiently secured to the costume.

Prohibited Weapons

Prohibited weapons include, but are not limited to:

Metal swords that cannot be secured in a sheath.
Flail weapons.
Bats and clubs, including baseball bats, golf clubs cricket
    bats and hockey sticks.
Incendiary or ignition weapons.
Self-defense weapons such as pepper spray, stun-guns, and
    Tasers.

If you are unsure if your weapon violates policy, contact the event organizers before the event.

PART II

AT THE EVENT

CHAPTER THREE

GENERAL CON RULES

- **RESPECT YOUR PEERS**
- **LINES! LINES! LINES!**
- **ITEMS TO BRING AND ITEMS TO LEAVE AT HOME**
- **CON ETIQUETTE IS NOT JUST A STATE**

While all conventions are run and operated a little differently from each other, there are some general rules that apply to most, if not all events.

RESPECT

By far the most important element of any convention, regardless of whether there are fifty attendees or 130,000, is respect. Respect your fellow attendees, respect the guests, respect the event staff and respect yourself. Everyone in the building is wanting the same experience and to end the day with a smile on their face. The event will be far more enjoyable if you remember that you are not the only attendee there and that your behavior can affect others.

The typical rules of social decorum apply.

- Do not cut in line
- No pushing or shoving
- No bullying
- No stealing or shoplifting
- Do not interfere with cosplayer's costumes
- Do not get drunk or high
- No loud cursing (kids are present)
- No inappropriate costumes
- No fighting
- No sad faces (hey, it is a convention, leave that frown at home)

Many of these rules are covered in greater detail elsewhere in the book.

WE DON'T NEED NO STINKING BADGES

Your ticket is your key to the kingdom. Without it, you're not going to be able to set foot in the venue. The ticket is generally in the form of a printed out ticket, a badge or a wrist strap, so you are easily identifiable to the numerous security guards as someone who belongs there.

When you pick up the ticket, you are agreeing to the rules of the convention and violation of the rules can result in forfeit of its privileges. These rules are available on the event's website and are usually printed on the back of the ticket.

Keep in mind that you are also agreeing to allow the event, its agents, or assignees to use your image and/or likeness for advertising or promotion by the event for this and future events. Be warned, you may find your face plastered across future fliers and websites.

Your badge must be worn at all times and must be visible

to security. If your badge cannot be viewed, be prepared to be stopped regularly. Yes, I know it may not go with your costume, but after the tenth time of being stopped going into the vendor hall, you'll give up and put it on display. The irritation of it not matching your costume will be far less than the inconvenience of being stopped at every door. Individuals without badges will be stopped by security and not allowed into the convention.

Badges are usually non-replaceable, so if you lose it, you're done. While this may sound unfair, because badges don't have individual names on them, there is no proof you didn't just give your badge to a non-paying attendee.

DON'T FORGET YOUR LINES

One of the unfortunate byproducts of any convention and an issue you will see rampant, especially at the larger conventions is lines. You will spend a good portion of your time just waiting in line. Be prepared to line up everywhere.

- You will line up to get in
- You will line up for food
- You will line up to check out at vendors
- You will line up for panels
- You will line up to get event exclusives
- You will line up to meet celebrities
- You will line up for the bathroom
- You will line up to get cash
- You will line up to get out
- Then, when you get to your car, you will line up to get out of the parking lot

Odds are you may even find yourself standing in a line and you have no idea why.

At some events, these lines can last for hours. The cold, hard truth is lines are as much a part of comicon and conventions as celebrities and costumes and at some point during the event, you are going to find yourself standing in line.

Mind Your Manners

The usual rules apply for lines at conventions. No cutting and no holding spots for ten of your friends. It is not fair for the people standing behind in line. They may not be able to get into a particular part of the event or get an exclusive item if you are the place holder for thirty of your closest buddies.

To help with this issue, more and more events are starting to issue tickets to the more popular panels and programming to help alleviate the crowds that line up. It is incredibly disappointing to spend three hours in line only to find out that the room filled up three people ahead of you.

Remember the section about showering? This is where it becomes vital to your neighbor's enjoyment. If someone is standing next to you for two hours, make sure you smell fresh.

Line Buddies

Once you're in line, you could find yourself there for a while. Reach out and make friends. Conventions and comicons are social events, so be social. Chances are, they have the same interests as you and the three hour wait in line will suddenly fly by. Besides, if you need to run to the bathroom or go get a snack, you now have someone to hold your place and a friendly face to return to.

CHILDREN

The majority of conventions allow children to attend. The general rule is all children age 12 and under must be accompanied by an adult all times.   Many conventions let young children enter for free with a paid adult, but they will likely still need a badge.

Curfew

If you are bringing children, become familiar with the curfew laws of the city as they may vary state by state. Curfew hours usually apply seven days a week, year round.

PETS AND ANIMALS

Service and assistance animals are usually permitted at the venue, but again, your safest bet is to double check with customer service venue first.   No other animals will be permitted in the convention space even if they are a part of your costume.

LOITERING

Walking around a convention for hours on end can get tiring. When you need a rest, find a designated area and take a load off for a few minutes. Do not camp out in a hallway or in front of a door where you can be a trip hazard.   Keep in mind that not everyone is in costume has a large field of vision and can easily step on or trip over you and that won't end well for anyone.

DO NOT PULL THE FIRE ALARM

This one sounds like common sense, but it happens.   I've been at events where the fire alarm has been pulled and while the fire department and venue staff handled it very well, it is huge downer and many decide to simply go home and cut the day short.

It affects everyone involved in the event.   The vendors are forced to leave their booths, celebrities and fans are forced to go and stand outside, sometimes in the middle of summer, waiting for the all clear to go back inside.

Depending on who you believe, the alarms may or may not have a security device built into them that will spray either colored or UV ink onto your hands. If this does indeed happen and you are caught, charges will very likely be pressed for being a public nuisance. Safely evacuating 75,000 people is not a task to be taken lightly.

WI-FI WHAT SPOTS?

I've lost count of the venues where Wi-Fi or cell phone coverage is not readily available. This is especially the case if the venue has levels located below ground. Do not expect to have a signal every minute you are at the event, you will likely find numerous dead spots throughout the venue. Be sure to set your phone to Airplane mode. Eight hours of searching for a signal will play havoc on your battery's life and when you really need it; your phone will be dead. If you didn't remember to bring your charger with you, you're on a communication blackout until you can get to one.

FOOTWEAR

Make sure you have suitable footwear. You will be amazed at how much walking you'll be doing over the course of the weekend. Your feet will be very grateful that you didn't wear heels or flip flops.

ITEMS TO BRING

I.D.

Make sure you have your I.D. with you. You may need it when you check in. Additionally, if you intend to drink or buy R rated movies, you will probably get carded.

Backpack

While backpacks can be a life saver when you start grabbing freebies and buying merchandise, be mindful of those around you. They can get full and heavy very quickly and it is easy to smack someone in the face when turning around.

Hand Sanitizer

When you've been sandwiched in a building with 80,000 of your closest friends, chances are you are going to run into someone who is sick, is getting sick or has just been sick. The chances are also good of you catching it. Keep your hands clean and sanitized as much as possible.

Vitamins

Before you go to an event, be sure to stock up on vitamin C, Airborne and other immune system boosters. There are all kinds of wonderful germs floating around.

Camera

Don't forget your camera. From the moment you enter the convention, there will be dozens, if not hundreds of opportunities to snap photos at every turn. From cosplayers, to celebrities to interactive sets, you will find no shortage of subjects. Make sure your camera is charged and the memory card has plenty of space on it.

Snacks

Eating meals and especially snacking at a convention can get expensive very quickly. Bring some snacks with you so that you don't over pay at snack vendors.

Refillable Water Bottle

As previously mentioned, you will be doing a lot of walking. Make sure you stay hydrated throughout the day. Most venues will have water fountains available. Bringing your own bottle allows for faster and cheaper refills.

Medical Kit

If you have room in your back or purse, consider bringing some basic medical supplies such as aspirin, tissues, Band-Aids and Chap Stick. Chances are you won't need them, but they take up little space in your bag.

Deodorant/Antiperspirants

You won't think about this until you stand next to someone in line who isn't wearing any. Your next stop will be the bathroom to apply a refresh coat, just to be safe.

Device Power

If you have room, make sure you bring a power supply for your wireless devices. You will need your phone charged to ensure you can regroup with party members, take photos and get updates via mobile apps and social networking. Consider purchasing an external battery to prolong your device's life.

ITEMS TO LEAVE AT HOME

Only bring the necessities with you. Items can get easily lost at conventions. If it isn't essential to the event, leave it at home. You don't want to dig into your backpack and drop something on the floor. You will not enjoy your weekend if you have to go and buy a new laptop on Monday because you dropped it.

Electronics

If you don't need your tablet or laptop, it is safer to leave it at home. It will weigh down your backpack and could hurt someone if they bump into you. Unless you are hosting a panel, bringing your laptop is generally a bad idea. You will also have to line up to get your bag searched when you first enter.

Loaded Weapons

Regardless of open carry laws, most conventions will not let you bring a loaded weapon into the venue. Leave your ammunition at home.

Stroller

As a parent, I understand having to bring a small child to an event when there is not a sitter available. While you can technically bring in a stroller, the people around you will thank you if you don't. Strollers are not battering rams and should not be used for a clearing a path through the masses. Consider using a sling or similar type of device to carry your child. There is only so much available floor space in a venue, so try to keep your footprint as reasonable as possible.

Better yet, if the child is an infant, you may just be better off trying to find a sitter and leaving the little one at home. There is a chance they could get smooshed or bumped in the crowds. Not to mention if you have to line up to get into a bathroom with a fussy baby, you're going to have a mess on your hands.

The Grumpy Friend

If you have a friend who really doesn't want to go to a

convention, do everyone a favor and leave them at home. They will be happier for it, you will be happier for it and the people who would have to listen to them complain the entire time will be happier for it.

Conventions are about having fun. No one wants to listen to someone complaining about lines, food prices or making fun of people in costumes. If you or one of your party doesn't want to be there, don't go. We've all been to a concert or movie and heard someone complaining through its entirety. It gets really tiresome very quickly.

NO LOUD MUSIC OR DANCING

As much fun as impromptu dance and song parties are, the convention hall is not the place to have one. Be considerate of people around you and keep the volume down and save the Footloose cravings for later.

ALCOHOL

Some venues serve alcohol on the premises to attendees with a valid picture I.D. The usual rules apply to purchasing alcohol.

Don't supply alcohol to minors. Don't use a fake I.D. to purchase alcohol. Don't drink and drive.

Don't drink to the point you can't stand and are barfing all over the floor. The cleaning crew have enough garbage to clean up during the event without you biohazarding all over the place.

DRUGS

Do I really need to say to not bring or do drugs to a convention? Yes? Don't.

CHAPTER FOUR

AT THE CONVENTION

- **GETTING AROUND**
- **STAYING WITH YOUR PARTY**
- **PLAYING WELL WITH OTHERS**
- **LOST AND FOUND**

So the big day is finally here. Get ready, because the next few days are going to be really exciting and exhausting. Make sure you get plenty of sleep the night before. You will be running on adrenalin for a while, but once that wears off, you will crash fast if you haven't been sleeping at the end of the day. Between balls and after parties, it is very easy to find yourself still going strong eighteen hours later.

NAVIGATING THE FLOOR

Make your way into the main doors at a reasonable speed. You may be picking your jaw up at the sight of the main convention hall, but if you stop dead in your tracks, all you are doing is blocking traffic and someone is very likely to slam into your back.

The main convention floor can be an incredibly busy and frustrating place. You will see a seemingly endless line of people slowly moving around the hall. Trying to cross these lines can be almost impossible. If you need to get to the opposite end of the room, you may want to consider stepping out into the corridor. The crowds are thinner and you can get around much faster.

SENDING OUT THE SEARCH PARTY

With thousands of people at a convention, it is very easy to get separated from your party, assuming of you course you came with one. You can spend hours wandering around trying to find the rest of your group. Before you get to the convention, decide on a location that you will meet, if and when you get separated. If you can, make it one of the first places you visit when you arrive so the group is familiar with its location.

YOU CAN'T ALWAYS GET WHAT YOU WANT

Any convention with more than a few thousand attendees means that you will not be able to do everything you want to do. You will not be able to meet every celebrity and you will not be able to attend every panel. It is just the nature of the beast.

As mentioned previously, before you arrive, get familiar with the schedule. Start making a conquest list to determine which panels and celebrities are the most important to you. Allow time to get to these panels and celebrity booths. In many cases you will not be able to simply walk in a few minutes before the panel starts and get a seat, especially with the more popular celebrities. In some cases you will have to line up for a few hours to guarantee yourself a spot. In this time you may be able to do two or three other smaller events instead.

HAVE A PLAN B

The plan for the weekend you just made in the previous chapter? Make another one. You are going to be very disappointed if you make a main list and don't get to do anything on it. Make sure you have a backup plan to ensure you still get value out of the event. If you spend your entire time lining up for panels you don't end up getting into, you are not going to leave with the fondest of memories. How much fun you have depends on you. Also, remember that the overflow hotels may also have programming and events in their ballrooms and meeting rooms,

PACE YOURSELF

One of the most important factors of the convention is taking care of yourself. Eat well, drink plenty, take vitamins and get sleep. You don't want to get to the end of the event only to be so exhausted and run down that you can't get out of bed. A lot can be said for pacing yourself. Remember, this is not a race, it is a marathon.

Stop by the celebrity autograph area and check out the lines. If the line at one of the guest's booths is short and they are on your to-do list, take care of it now. You have no way of knowing if the line is going to be worse later in the day.

KEEP MOVING

One of the biggest irritants at an event is the person who sees something of interest and just stops dead in their tracks. This is the easiest way to get stepped on or bumped into. Do not just stop in the middle of an aisle. Be mindful of the crowd around you and the flow of foot traffic. If something catches your attention, move out of the way of traffic and go check it out. You don't like to be stepped on and most people won't like stepping on you. It is important to keep the flow of traffic moving as much as possible.

NO YELLING

Yelling "Hey!" into the crowd will make everyone around you stop and turn to see if you are looking for them. Shouting "Hey, Josh!" will make less people turn around, but people will still stop. The convention hall can get loud; yelling is not an effective method of communication. Either use your phone or reconvene at your predetermined meeting place. The event is loud enough as it is with ambient chatter and energy, don't add to it unnecessarily.

MANNERS

Remember, *Please, thank you* and *you're welcome* go a long way, especially if you are in a large crowd. Excitement and awe are not excuses to be rude or forget your manners. If anything, it is the opposite and you need manners now more than ever.

If you bump into someone and spill their drink or cause them to drop their food a simple "sorry" isn't going to cut it. Certainly don't ignore them. Offer to replace their item. A good show of manners will go a long way. If you're not looking where you are going and you walk into someone, it is not fair to expect them to pick up the tab to replace their food. Especially with the price of convention food.

Also don't snatch items that others have picked up at vendor's booths. Far too many times I have seen someone pick up something desirable only to have someone else snatch it out of their hands.

MISSING BELONGINGS

Conventions are not responsible for items lost on the premises, so be mindful of this before you take your $600 iPhone with you.

Many events and venues have a lost and found area, so if something does come up missing, check to see if it has been handed in.

While I'd love to say that there is no chance of crime at an event, if you are surround by 100,000 people, chances are one or two are going to be a little on the iffy side. Do not leave personal belongings unattended or valuables visible in pockets and purses. Nothing puts a dampener on your weekend faster than realize someone has lifted $500 out of your pocket. Be mindful of your belongings.

It isn't always a thief that is responsible for lost items. Sometimes you may just drop things and not realize it. Clean out your wallet or purse of all excess items that you don't need, such as extra credit cards, miscellaneous I.D.'s and whatnot. If you are unfortunate enough to lose your purse or wallet, it won't be a complete disaster. It is better to be safe than sorry. Losing all of your credit and debit cards on a Sunday is extremely inconvenient and will kill your convention plan dead in its tracks.

On the flip side, if you do happen to find someone else's property such as a phone or wallet, do the right thing and turn it in. Not only is it the right thing to do, it is good karma. Don't look for money or credit cards. Imagine it was you who was looking for your wallet or purse. You would be hoping and praying that someone did the right thing and turned it in. Pay it forward. You never know when you'll need to be on the receiving end of some good karma.

CHAPTER FIVE

VOLUNTEERING

- **THE ROLE OF THE VOLUNTEER**
- **AVAILABLE POSITIONS**
- **PAYMENT**
- **RELIABILITY**

*T*he vast majority of conventions rely on volunteers to help staff the event and ensure it runs smoothly. Anyone can sign up to be a volunteer, but before you do, become familiar with what it entails. Even though you are at a convention, it is still work. Most events will have details on their website for interested parties.

Volunteers are as important as any guest at a convention. Without them, the event would quickly fall into chaos. An event, especially the larger ones are like well-oiled machines and what you see on the surface as an attendee is only a small piece of a much larger puzzle.

As a volunteer, you need to be able to handle pressure. You

must remain professional at all times and remember you are dealing with people with a large variety of beliefs, ages, genders and health conditions, both physical and mental. Treat every attendee with respect and consideration even if given reason to do so otherwise.

VOLUNTEERS ARE PEOPLE TOO

Be mindful that regardless of whether you are attending as a fan, a guest or are volunteering yourself, volunteers are usually nothing more than fans giving their time to help the event. Everyone at a convention wants to have a good time. No one wants to be miserable. If something isn't going the way you want, yelling at the staff fixes nothing. Remember, most of the volunteers at conventions are fans just like you and me. Their reward for volunteering is a ticket to the event, not a huge paycheck.

POSITIONS

There are many roles within a convention that require volunteers. These roles include staffing events leading up to the convention and also the days of the convention. Depending on the size of the convention, some require volunteers for a few weeks after the event has ended. Volunteer roles include but are not limited to:

GENERAL EVENT STAFF

These are the staff that help with the core functions of running a convention.

Ticketing Booth/Check In

Fans entering the venue will need to pay for or pick up badges. Volunteers will help guests get registered and into the event.

Line Management

As discussed earlier, lines and conventions go together like peanut butter and jelly. Line management volunteers make sure that attendees get to their destination without blocking aisles and exits. Please be patient with line staff, sometimes lines grown at an astounding rate and there can be some teething problems while the line is reorganized.

Programming

Programming at a convention doesn't come together on its own. Depending on the size of the convention, program management may be broken down into genres and require a different staff member for each category. The smaller conventions will likely have one or two staff covering multiple genres.

Clean Up and Tear Down

As with any event, the job doesn't end when the last person has left the floor. Many conventions will need help with cleaning up the event hall and ensuring the place is left in the same condition it was found.

Celebrity Chaperone

Many conventions rely on volunteers to help pick up celebrities from the airport, get them to the event and shuttle them around the city after the event has finished. You will generally be reimbursed for gas and mileage if you are providing your own vehicle. Background checks may be required for this role.

This is a role you have to earn and you will likely not start out driving A-List celebrities around. As you build up trust and a good reputation, you will likely work with more famous celebrities.

Do not expect to be given Stan Lee on your first outing.

MARKETING

Public Outreach

The street team is a very important aspect of any convention. These are the troops who take to the streets and spread the word of the upcoming event. You can't just plan a convention and expect people to know about it and show up. The hard part is making people aware of it and getting them through the doors. This is now much harder due to the influx of conventions sweeping the planet.

It simply is not enough to jump online, throw together a website and spam your Facebook friends with event invites. More than half the time those invites go to people out of state who probably do not have the desire or ability to attend. I've lost track of the number of Facebook invites I've received to events on the opposite end of the continent and foreign countries. The street team generates a buzz in the host town or city and the surrounding area.

Street team activities can include, but are not limited to, passing out fliers and staffing booths at other events and being seen around town. Your job is to make as many people aware of the event as possible. Without attendees, conventions can get boring very quickly.

Information Desk

The Information Desk is the front line for information related to the event. Attendees will flood to the information booth looking for such things as bathrooms, food, programming rooms, and the location of various celebrities. Knowing the layout of the event will help desperate convention fans trying to find a particular room or event as they rush around.

MODERATORS

Moderators are used in the various panels and presentations held during the event. Responsibilities include introducing guests, selecting questions from the audience and keeping things on schedule. Moderating is discussed in greater detail in chapter ten.

TECHNOLOGY

Photo Booth Staff

Many events have photo booths set up for both celebrity and candid photo opportunities of attendees. Responsibilities include selling photo ops to attendees, answering questions and getting photo's ready for pickup. Volunteers may also assist with helping attendees through the photo process. After event responsibilities may include uploading images to a host website or e-mailing images to attendees.

Technical

All of the presentations that you see at a convention did not magically set themselves up. Information Technology and Audio Video staff work feverishly behind the scenes to set them up. Not all venues provide in-house AV or IT staff to set up and monitor audio/video equipment, so tech staff volunteers become a valuable commodity.

Volunteers should have computer and AV experience for on-site technical responsibilities. This includes setting up equipment, tearing it down after the event has finished and any necessary troubleshooting that may occur.

Payment

Volunteering is exactly what it implies, volunteering your time for free.

Gratis.

Nada.

Most conventions will provide you with a day pass to the event as a thank you for volunteering and that's it.

Now, on saying that, there are a few roles that are paid positions. It is up to you to make sure you know exactly what you are getting into before signing up. Do not work an event expecting payment where none is due. You will get to Sunday evening and not be a happy camper.

BE RELIABLE

If you are volunteering at an event, make sure you arrive on time, so that you can be at your assigned place as the schedule dictates. If you are late or simply don't bother to show, you can affect the schedule for most of the day.

If you volunteer, shy of sickness or family emergency, there is no excuse to just not show up. If you can't commit, don't commit. A convention is a machine of many parts. It is only as good as the people running it. If twenty people decide to not show the day of the event, the entire convention could be thrown into chaos.

VOLUNTEER AGREEMENT

Most conventions will have a volunteer agreement that all volunteers will be required to sign prior to being able to work the event.

CHAPTER SIX

SHOPPING

- ● BRING CASH
- ● EVENT EXCLUSIVES
- ● IMPULSE SHOPPING
- ● GETTING THE BEST DEAL

When you're at a convention, you are going to spend money and quite possibly a lot of it. After all, why else are you there? The odds of you being able to leave the event empty handed are slim. In fact, you may want to check for a pulse if you do. With an almost endless supply of vendors selling their wares from every genre and medium under the sun, you will be hard pressed to find something that doesn't appeal to you.

The vendor floor is going to be full of booths selling almost everything you can imagine. You'll find t-shirts, posters, toys, artwork and movie props. There will be, signed books, rare movies and fan made props such as fez's, Jayne hats, Dr. Who corsets and custom lightsabers among many others. If you want it, chances are there is someone selling it. If you are at a genre-specific event, the vendor wares will be even more custom tailored to your interests, focusing on the core theme of the event. The reality is, every which way you turn, there will be places to spend money.

THIS IS GONNA GET EXPENSIVE

Think of a convention as you would a sporting event, concert or Disneyland. Once you get in the door, almost everything is three times the price it is outside. This may not be true for vendors, but for staples like food and drink, you'll be paying movie theater prices for a bottle of water.

This isn't saying it is right or wrong to charge more at events; it is just how it is. People are there to make money. Be aware of this before you arrive. You don't want to end up starving because you didn't budget an extra $40 to eat and drink during the day. $40 sounds a lot, but if you get there early you could be at the event for ten hours. In that time you'll want lunch and will snack throughout the day. It will add up fast and if it is a multi-day event, you could easily end up spending over $100 just in food and water. Either bring sufficient funds to cover this or bring snacks and a bottle of water to tide you through until lunch or dinner.

Remember, your badge does give you in and out privileges. You are not tethered to the venue for eating and drinking. Is it convenient to eat there? Sure, but you'll be paying for that convenience heavily.

CASH IS KING

While using credit cards can be very convenient, having cash on you can be beneficial for a number of reasons.

Many vendors are likely to adjust their pricing if you can

pay cash. This saves them from having to pay credit card fees and they can pass the savings directly on to you. Cash allows you to barter a little.

Bring some smaller bills too. Paying in smaller bills will make vendors even happier. Don't drop a $100 bill on a $3 action figure five minutes after getting on the floor. If a vendor runs out of change, they are effectively shut down until they can get more. There is a good chance they would refuse the sale in a case like that. Carry plenty of $1's, $5's and $10's.

Some vendors are cash only. This may be due to limited Wi-Fi or dealing in low priced items.

Most celebrities allow for payment of autographs and photographs directly at their booths and most are cash only. With Wi-Fi rates varying in cost and 4G reception sketchy at best, cash will get you out of the booth faster and cheaper. Remember that whole section on lines? This is one of those times when they can be avoided.

As previously mentioned, try to avoid on-site ATM's. If you are unable to get to the bank before the event and if you have to use one of the on-site ATM's, be prepared to pay heavily for the convenience.

BUDGET CON

Set yourself a reasonable budget and try your best to stick to it. While convention owners love for you to spend money and have a good time, they don't want you to do it at the cost of getting evicted from your home because you just had to buy a life sized Han Solo in Carbonite. You don't want to be checking your bank account Monday morning and realizing you have more fingers than dollars in the bank. Han may look really good in the corner, but he's not going to keep the electricity turned on or a roof over your head.

THE VENDOR HALL

Shopping is one of the most exciting elements of Comicon. When entering the vendor and exhibitor hall, you will walk into a wall of literally hundreds of vendors. They will carry everything and anything you could want related to pop culture and your genres of interest.

CHECK THE PRICE

One of the easiest traps to fall into in the vendor hall is overpaying for an item during a spur of the moment impulse purchase. We've all done it. You walk into a vendor's booth and see something you've had your eye on for a while and bought it, only to get home to find it cheaper on eBay. Much, much cheaper. Granted, online shopping has taken much of the fun out of the hunt when tracking down items, but it has also created significant competition in the market.

It is easy to get excited when you finally get to hold a rare item in your hands, but if you are not careful, you can quickly find yourself paying far more than what you would have done outside the convention. Seeing something up close is a lot different than browsing through images online, but a little research beforehand can save you buyer's remorse once you've gone home.

Personally, I am a Star Wars action figure collector and there are usually dozens of vendors selling figures from the various lines Kenner and Hasbro have released over the years. While it is impossible to find every figure in stores, it is possible to find them on various online resellers such as eBay and other sellers.

Anytime I go to a convention, I take a list of a dozen or so figures I am curious about and jot down the ballpark values that I find online. That way I have a reference to go back to if I see the figures I'm looking for.

KNOW THE MARKET

Of course, there are times when you are quite obviously staring at a bargain. I was at a convention recently and one of the sellers was blowing out carded Star Wars figures from the 2000 - 2009 lines two for $5. I didn't need eBay to know that Luke Skywalker in Sandstorm gear and General Veers for $2.50 was a screaming deal. So were the other fifty or so figures I picked up. This was a no brainer and I promptly loaded up my arms and grabbed as many as I could. Knowing I had holes in my collection I wanted to fill.

However, this meant I had to walk back to my car much earlier than I was expecting, otherwise I'd be carrying six bags around with me for the rest of the day. Even smart shopping can have its drawbacks. Remember that line about pacing yourself and not parking too far away? Yeah... There is nothing like having to stumble a mile back to your car in the mid-day sun with your arms loaded with bags because you parked at the wrong end of the venue.

By the end of the first day, they had been picked clean, so the inconvenience was worth it.

IS IT RARE?

If you see something that you know is readily available at a Walmart or Toys R' Us near to your house, determine if it is really worth buying. You may be better off saving your money for something a bit more exclusive to the event. Part of the fun of checking out vendors at a convention is seeing new, exclusive and rare items up close and personal.

Also, be sure to research key items that you know you will be looking for before the convention. Check on eBay and other online toy stores such as Brian's Toys, Big Bad Toy Store, Entertainment Earth, Dork Side Toys to name but a few. A little preemptive homework can save you from a lot of heartache when you get home. Being stuck with an item you significantly overpaid sucks the fun out of it really quickly.

PLAN AHEAD

If you know you're going to be buying comic books, bring some bags and boards to ensure your exclusive comics get home in mint condition. While this is a staple of comic book collecting, not all sellers carry boards and bags in their booths. Additionally, if you are expecting to buy a poster or piece of artwork, bring a poster mailing tube to avoid damage. If you collect action figures and don't care about them being on the card, bring Ziploc bags to store the loose figures in. This makes carrying multiple figures far easier.

BE PATIENT

Unless you know you're getting a terrific bargain or that the item is an absolute rarity, don't buy the first thing you see. It is very easy to walk up to the first booth you come across and spend all your money on an impulse buy. Pace yourself, if you're staying for the entire weekend, you could have upwards of thirty hours left for you to find something else even cooler or even better, much cheaper.

You will find two types of vendors at these events. There are the vendors who are looking to clear out inventory and off-load goods at much discounted prices and the vendors charging premium prices. Shop around before making a commitment on a high ticket item. Not all vendors price their items equally.

EVENT EXCLUSIVES

Many events have exclusive items available to attendees. These could be comic books, art prints, action figures or any number of collectible items. These items are designed to be exclusive for the attendees and are usually very limited in quantity. If you are fortunate enough to be able to pick up one, just pick up ONE. Buying multiples to turn around and hawk on the secondary markets is bad for two reasons.

First, it defeats the purpose of event exclusives. Second, it limits the inventory available to other fans at the event who want one for themselves and their own collections. Hasbro generally has exclusive Star Wars figures available at San Diego Comicon and you can go on eBay during the event and see hundreds of said figure going online for five or ten times the price. Yes, it is frustrating for non-attendees to not have access to these items due to their exclusive nature, but it is more frustrating for an actual attendee who is there in person and is unable to obtain one because of scalpers. Be considerate of others attendee's wants. The convention is not about lining your own pockets.

Many event exclusives cost a little more than regular priced items, but due to the exclusive nature of the item, it is very likely to hold its value.

FREEBIES

It is entirely possible to go to a convention and leave with a bag full of swag and not pay a single dime.

Many vendors give away freebies such as t-shirts, buttons and posters to promote new and upcoming books and movies. Additionally, many events will have a large swag table with stacks of full size and mini movie posters for you to take home. Most of these are usually of movies released at least six months ago. However, if you look hard enough, you may be able to find some real hidden treasures.

Moderation

Do not just grab freebies just for the sake of grabbing them. If it isn't something that genuinely interests you, leave it for someone who wants it. Just because something is free, it does not mean you need to take it.

Also, don't take items with the goal of flipping on eBay. The studios are nice enough to hand out items for free. Don't take stacks to turn a quick profit on. Let everyone at the event have the chance to get one.

PURCHASING WEAPONS

The same rules about bringing weapons into the venue will apply here. If you purchase a weapon it will either need to be peace bonded immediately or removed from the event entirely, if security is unable to tag it. Consider this when making a weapon purchase.

Some vendors may be nice enough to hold the item for you until the end of the day, depending on the size of the booth and the amount of sales they are making. They don't have unlimited storage, so don't count on this always being an option.

BEFORE LEAVING

Don't forget to pick up any items vendors may be holding for you. It is not their fault if you forget. Remember that not all vendors are located in-town. Some may be packing up and heading to a different state at the end of the event. You will then likely have to pay shipping if you are unable to pick it up.

CHAPTER SEVEN

PHOTOGRAPHS

- ● *PHOTO ETIQUETTE*
- ● *GETTING THE BEST PICTURES*
- ● *BEING PHOTOGRAPHED*
- ● *WHAT TO AVOID*

*I*f you've brought a camera with you, then you are going to have ample opportunity to snap pictures. Conventions are a wonderful place for photographers, both amateur and professional alike. Between costumes and cosplayers, displays, props, obscure merchandise, panels, friends and celebrities, you'll be draining your phone or camera's battery and filling its memory card in no time at all.

As with all elements of attending a convention, there some general items of etiquette to consider when taking photographs of other attendees, both in and out of costume. It isn't just a case of pointing and shooting any time you feel like it.

TAKING A PICTURE WITH A COSTUMER

Always be mindful of boundaries when taking a picture with a costumer. Ask if it is okay if you put your arm around them.

Under no circumstances ever, EVER grab private parts, butts or breasts on men or women. This is sexual assault and can and does lead to arrest. Harassment, bullying and inappropriate behavior is covered in further detail in Chapter Eleven.

TAKING PHOTOGRAPHS

Photograph Etiquette

When you find something you want to take a photograph of, make sure you are not blocking aisles or doors. Many booths and costuming groups will have large prop displays for you to interact with. You can easily cause a backup behind you if you stop dead in your tracks in the middle of an aisle to take photos. You are likely to get bumped into if you stop in front of a large crowd and your pictures will probably turn out blurry. Worse case, you may drop your camera. Always be aware of your surroundings.

Photographing Celebrities

Avoid taking candid photos of celebrities while they are sitting at their booths. The same rules apply to snapping shots of celebrities as they do for photographing guests in costumes, ask first. Most celebrities charge a nominal fee to meet them and have your picture taken with them.

Photographing Cosplayers

Before taking a photograph of any attendee, ensure your

camera or cell phone is turned on and ready to go. Don't spend thirty seconds tweaking settings, as the subject may start to get agitated, especially if others are hounding them for a photo at the same time, which is quite often the case.

The universal rule for taking photos of attendees in costumes is to ask first. You will find that people are far more receptive if you just simply ask. A little courtesy can go a long way. While most people in costume at the event love the attention and fully expect it, there are some who many not be comfortable in front of a camera. Always ask first, even though nine times out ten the answer will be yes. A simple "May I take your picture, please?" is all you need. If you recognize the character, adding the name into your query will give you bonus points.

Make sure the subject is not busy or talking to another guest. Barging in and interrupting will not get you your picture any faster, if indeed at all.

Give the cosplayer some time to make any necessary adjustments to their costume and hide their badge. Moving about can shift pieces around. They will also likely want to pose for the photo. Countdown before taking a picture so they can be sure they are ready.

Getting the Perfect Picture

It is common courtesy to ask if the costumer can move out of the aisle to prevent backup. If you are close to a wall, it would provide a better backdrop for the picture, but do not expect a costumer to move to the other end of the venue so you can get a better photo. Always be aware of any inconvenience to the costumer.

Many people in costume will automatically pose when a camera is put in front of them, but if they do not, feel free to politely ask if they would pose and get into character. Make sure to give them quick and clear direction, so you aren't frustrating them. They also want to enjoy the convention and not spend hours posing for photographers who aren't sure of the photo they want to take. If you can communicate your intentions, then they can assist in helping you get the shot you are looking for.

It is okay if you want to take a couple of shots, but be considerate to not only the costumer's time, but also that of the other attendees. There will be others wanting to take photos and if everyone took a minute to take the picture, the costumer would spend the entire convention posing and many others would not be able to get a picture. Try to wrap up the entire process in five to ten seconds. If you mess up the shot, forget it and move to the next person. Use the lesson to not repeat the same mistake.

Photographing Children

If you are going to be taking a photo of a child in costume, always ask the parent's permission first. ***Always***. If the parent says no, respect their wishes, politely say thank you and find another subject. Many children dress up in costume because they want to, not because they or their parent wants their picture taken. The rules differ from that of an adult. Please be aware of this at all times.

Respect the Costumer

Remember, there are real people under these costumes. Some of these costumes get hot, very hot and the costumer can get uncomfortable. They get tired, hungry and thirsty. Eight hours in costume may not seem like a lot, but it can be extremely exhausting.

They are not at your beck and call to pose at your command.

If you see someone sitting down with their helmet or mask off, please be considerate and let them rest. Telling them they are letting your child down and ruining the convention for them because they are taking a break is not fair. This is not Disneyland. People in costume are not paid actors or mascots; they are there to share their love of a particular character or franchise with the public. They pose for pictures out of kindness. They are not on a schedule and do not perform on demand. Cut them some slack. Shouting at them or making them feel bad doesn't help anyone. If you wait patiently for a few minutes, you will find that most costumers will soon be back in character and back on the floor ready for more photo ops.

Don't Be Weird

Don't say things to a costumer that could make them feel uncomfortable. At a recent event, I was in my Stormtrooper armor taking a selfie with an attendee and he whispers into my helmet "Your armor is worthless. If I shoot you in the heart with my .45, you'll die pretty quickly". He taps what I hoped to be a toy pistol on his belt.

Thanks, dude. Now I need to run away from you as fast as I can. If you are the fellow who said this, don't. It is creepy.

Respect the Costume

A vast majority of costumes at a convention are handmade by the person wearing it. Please consider this before getting physical in a photo op. Many costumes are not designed to be aggressively man-handled and pieces can easily break off if you're not careful. There is nothing more disheartening for a costumer to see a piece snap off of your costume because someone has been rough with you. Ask if you can put your arm around them before doing so. It is impossible to stress test a costume for every type of scenario before an event. Don't be that person who sends a costumer running to the bathroom in tears or fuming because you snapped an expensive part of their costume.

In some cases, mobility is also very limited outside of walking, so you may not always be able to get the pose you want. Ask the person in the costume if they are comfortable with a specific pose before assuming they can do it. Something as trivial as bending down is a challenge for some costumes. Sitting or kneeling down can be downright impossible for others.

As an attendee it is very easy to get caught up in the excitement of seeing a favorite costume or character walking around. Be patient and considerate and you will have your photo op.

Do not grab at pieces of costumes as costumers walking by to get their attention. This is the fastest way to upset them. The momentum of walking against the jerk of being pulled back can easily break pieces off of their costume.

BEING PHOTOGRAPHED

On the flip side of taking photographs, there is costumer etiquette when responding to a photograph request.

If you are in a costume, people will naturally want to take your picture and if it is a really good costume, you will be stopped every few feet to pose. It is understandable that this can get irritating at times, but this is the responsibility that comes with wearing a costume. Anything you want to do will take you ten times as long. A simple task such as walking to the bathroom can take thirty minutes or more if you're in an impressive costume.

Never be rude or yell at someone who asks you for a photo

if you don't feel like having one taken, regardless if it as an adult or child. There is rarely ill intent when asking for a photo. If you're heading to the bathroom and are in a rush, politely state that you are taking a brief break and will be back in five minutes. It is important to take care of yourself at events, but be considerate of other's feelings too.

Drink plenty, eat and rest as needed. Most people will be respectful of you and your time, if you are polite. Remember, there is a chance that your costume represents an idol for a young child. Your actions can have a dramatic effect on them. An eight year old boy does not want to be shouted at by Batman because you need the bathroom. There is a lot of social responsibility when wearing a costume at an event attended by children.

WHEN TO NOT TAKE A PHOTO

While there are ample opportunities to snap photos at a convention, there are also times, when discretion is needed and pictures should not be taken. Use your best judgment; costumers are not there for your entertainment.

If you've seen someone you think looks ridiculous in their costume, either how it is built or how it fits them, do not take their photograph to humiliate them on Facebook or Instagram. It is not cool and for the one or two people who will "like" the post and think it is funny, I guarantee more will think you are an ass for taking it and embarrassing the person.

If someone's already skimpy costume has shifted and they are unknowingly showing more skin than they realize, instead of leering and snapping a shot, politely let them know. They will appreciate the courtesy and you will be able to get the photo you wanted and everyone will be happy. Taking a picture of their costume in disarray is not just rude, it is really creepy.

If the person you wish to photograph is in mid conversation with another attendee, don't just take a candid picture. We tend to make some odd faces while talking. No one wants to be immortalized with their mouth wide open like they're catching flies. We've all had it done to us and it sucks.

If an attendee's costume has become stained or damaged during the event, they would most likely appreciate not having their photo taken while their costume is not at its best.

If someone photo bombs a photo and is making a crude gesture being your subject, delete the photo. Don't give the bomber their ten seconds of fame.

Do not take creeper photos under any circumstances. While the costumer may be showing cleavage, butt or abs, remember there is a complete costume to shoot. Do not just focus on specific parts of the anatomy, unless it is the face. If in doubt, a full body or head shot picture is the way to go. If you have to question whether a picture is in good taste, then chances are it isn't.

PROTECTING YOUR PHOTOS

Remember to download the pictures from your camera at the end of the day. This is important for two reasons.

If you were to lose your camera or phone, you won't lose all of the pictures you have taken during the event.

You won't suddenly run out of space on the memory card. With all of the sights and photo ops, you'll be amazed how quickly you can take 500 photos and fill up a 2GB memory card. Consider purchasing larger capacity cards.

CHAPTER EIGHT

Costuming

- **SUIT UP!**
- **INTERACTING WITH COSTUMERS**
- **WARDROBE MALFUNCTIONS**
- **GETTING AROUND SAFELY**

*C*onventions are synonymous with costumes and it is doubtful you will ever attend an event where you won't see at least one person decked out from head to toe as one of their favorite characters.

The great thing about conventions is that although you don't have to dress up to have fun, if you do, you will have a completely different experience. Costuming is one of the most exciting elements of any convention. This is where you can proudly wear your geek card on display for everyone to see. It is a time where you can walk into a room and cause heads to turn. Your costume can be a great conversation piece and people will swarm around you to take your picture.

Costumers spend countless hours working on detailed and accurate costumes to debut at events and some are so well done you'll swear they could have stepped off of the screen or from the pages of a comic book.

CAN ANYONE DRESS UP?

Yes! There is no secret society of costumers that you must be a member of to wear a costume. If you want to dress up, then do it. Fans from all walks of life come as their favorite pop culture icons and have a blast doing it.

As with all parts of conventions, there are rules to help make the experience an enjoyable one for both costumed and non-costumed attendees alike.

YOU MADE THAT?

You will see many types of costumes on the convention floor. Some will be off the shelf costumes purchased from retail stores like Walmart or Target, others from more dedicated costume stores. Some have been meticulously made by hand with high end materials and others may just be hand made on a budget and some people will just be wrapped in aluminum foil, but everyone is enjoying themselves.

LOOK BUT DON'T TOUCH

Some costumers spend hundreds, if not thousands of dollars on their costumes and take a lot of pride in their work, but no matter how well a costume is made, it can still break. If you are taking a photo with someone in costume, be gentle. I have had armor pieces break when someone has been a little over enthusiastic and bent me into a position I'm not supposed to be in. If you see a costume you admire, by all means approach the person and let them know. Costumers love hearing the impact their work has on other attendees.

Many of the costumes that you will see at the convention are hand made by the person wearing them. This is where you will find some of the most passionate fans. You will see superheroes, movie characters, anime characters, Steampunk fans and everything in between. The more genre specific events will likely have costumes tailored to that particular subcategory.

DO NOT SOUVENIR HUNT

Do not grab pieces of costumes for your own devices or entertainment. Not only is it extremely frustrating for the costumer, it can be very expensive to replace or repair damaged or missing parts, but there can be residual damage. Many costumers use their costumes for charity work such as visiting children's hospitals and fundraisers. Damaging or taking pieces of a cosplayer's costume takes that person out of commission until they can afford both the money and the time to repair the damage.

TEST YOUR COSTUME

Do not show up to an event having never fully tested your costume. This is important or a number of reasons.

You want to make sure the costume is strong enough to last a day of walking around. While obviously you can't test for eight hours straight, you can wear the costume for an hour around the house to see if pieces break or don't interact well. Designing a costume and wearing it all day are two very different things and there will be issues that arise that you just can't plan for.

You will want to determine how much mobility you have while wearing the costume. Something as trivial as bending down to greet a child can result in something snapping. Know your limitations.

Do any protruding pieces have sharp or unfinished edges that could snare and scratch other attendees? Yes, those giant Steampunk wings look really cool, but how likely are they to snag someone or hit them in the face when you walk by?

The most important thing to consider when wearing a costume is the safety of yourself and your fellow attendees. No one wants to get hurt because an attendee was careless or overzealous with their costume.

COSTUME WRANGLER

If you are in a costume where your movement or vision is limited, you will need to bring a costume wrangler to help guide you safely through the crowds. This isn't just for your own safety, but also for that of everyone around you. Without peripheral vision, it is easy to step on a child or walk into a display rack in a booth. Never mind the fact that you may have to go down an escalator or a flight of stairs. No one wants to see you making a grand entrance in an epic costume and diving face-first down two dozen steps. Although, if your goal is to be trending on Twitter, this is a great way to do it.

COSTUME COMMON SENSE

While conventions are built on the freedom to be who you are, you still need to exercise some caution and common sense when putting on a costume. For the most part, conventions and comicons are family events; therefore, the odds of seeing children there are high.

Avoid Costume Malfunctions

Make sure your costume is strong enough to support regular wear and tear. A costume malfunction in the middle of a crowded convention could be extremely embarrassing and if you have not brought a costume repair kit, the walk of shame back to your vehicle or hotel room could seem like a million miles.

People may get gropey and some may pull at strings and elastic. Sometimes laces snag and before you know it, your top has come loose and you are sharing yourself with the entire convention. No one wants to see you embarrassed.

Appropriate Cover

Make sure your costume is suitable for a family friendly environment. Of course there are many superheroes, villains and characters, both male and female that have skimpy and revealing costumes, but your costume should show no more skin that you would see at a beach or swimming pool. Body paint is not a suitable replacement.

Know Your Audience

While you do have the freedom to dress as any character you wish, know your audience. If you are going to a family friendly comicon and your thing is to dress up like a zebra and wear a giant black rubber appendage, you may be more at home at a fetish ball or adult event where that kind of costume would be more appropriate. Don't be that person who wears something offensive for the sake of being offensive. A parent should not have to explain what the dangly pieces are under a male My Little Pony character. Yes, I've had to do it with my three year daughter. "No! That is not Zecora! Step away from the creepy man with the big black rubber phallus who is trying to give you a hug".

Keep it PG. If you're unsure, err on the side of caution. There is no such thing as a costume being too family friendly.

Costume Footprint

If your costume has pieces that extend from it (wings, spikes, armor, etc.) or you are carrying a large prop, please be aware of your surroundings and of people around you. It is not the other person's fault if you spin around and clock them in the face with a giant set of wings. The larger conventions can have limited room on the convention floor for navigation. Make sure you have a reasonable footprint.

Footwear

Wear protective and smart footwear at all times. This means some sort of hard sole. Unitard or stocking feet are not sufficient. Not only will you be doing a lot of walking, your feet will be susceptible to injury.

Be comfortable in the shoes or footwear you are wearing. If you've never worn six inch heels before, a convention is probably not the best time to start. You will be doing a lot of walking over the course of the event. Crowds can get busy with escalators and stairs adding to the fray. If you get blisters on the first day, you are going to have a very long convention. Even if you go for just one day, bad footwear choices can make your day miserable.

Most conventions will not allow roller-skates, roller-blades or skateboards, inside the building. You may well have good control, but an elbow in the back and gravity will win every time.

COSTUME 911

At some point during the event, a part of your costume is probably going to break. This could happen from an overly excited fan grabbing hold of you when taking a picture or just the wear and tear of moving around the convention hall

all day. Try not to get aggressive if a fan accidently damages your costume. Chances are they didn't do it on purpose and feel terrible. Belittling them only makes the situation worse. If your costume has irreplaceable parts, seriously consider whether a convention is the ideal place to premiere it. Bad things can and do happen to good costumes.

REPAIR KIT

Bring a repair kit to the event to make emergency repairs if something breaks.

Batteries

If any part of your costume requires batteries, be it for aesthetics or function, make sure you carry extras. There is nothing worse than having fans die in a helmet and not having any AAA's on you. Trust me, I learned that one the hard way and on more than one occasion. If you find yourself going through batteries faster than you can buy them, consider buying rechargeable ones. They are more expensive up front, but will pay for themselves many times over.

Glue

E6000 and superglue are handy if a piece of your costume breaks off. However, you will need to give it some time to dry. If you are staying at a hotel, glue and clamp the broken piece when you get back to your room and you should be good to go the next day. Oh, yes, bring clamps.

Safety Pins

If a strap breaks or a button pops off, having safety pins will be a life saver. These can be the difference between fixing the costume and calling it quits for the day and going home.

CHAPTER NINE

CELEBRITIES/GUESTS

- **MEETING YOUR IDOLS**
- **AUTOGRAPHS AND PHOTO OPS**
- **SEEK OUT NEW TALENT**
- **ONE-ON-ONE**

One of the major selling points of a convention and one of the main reasons many people attend, is the guest list. The guests are celebrities and industry professionals who are associated with the genre or general theme of the convention. The bigger the convention gets, the larger the budget they have to spend on guests. As conventions get more popular, their power to draw bigger named celebrities increases significantly.

Depending on the size and popularity of the convention, the list of guests will range from obscure artists and authors to A-List Hollywood actors and actresses. The larger conventions will have a broad mix of known and lesser known guests. This provides a healthy balance so that fans don't spend the entire weekend in line for one person.

Intimate Opportunities

By all means, do not gloss over the smaller conventions thinking they are too small to have any decent guests. While they more than likely won't have high profile A-List celebrities, they are known to bring out niche genre guests from all kinds of franchises. Many of these guests are icons in their genre. These may be celebrities you admired as a kid or people you have long forgotten about. There is a very good chance that one of the guests is someone you've admired for a while.

While I love meeting the A-List guests, conventions of all sizes have given me wonderful memories. Some of my favorite convention moments have been at smaller conventions with lesser known guests. I have been able to meet some wonderful people and have memorabilia signed I've owned since I was a child. At a recent convention, I was able to meet a gentleman called John Russo. He was the screenwriter for the zombie movie classic *Night of the Living Dead* and author of *Return of the Living Dead*. I have owned the first edition book since I was seven and was finally able to get it signed and personalized. I was able to talk to him for almost half an hour. Smaller conventions allow for longer one on one time. Mr. Russo's works are what got me into writing. No one else came to the convention and had this exact experience. These kinds of personal moments are abundant at conventions with each attendee making their own memories.

MEETING CELEBRITIES

Remember, celebrities are just like you. They just have really cool jobs. They love meeting their fans; else they wouldn't be at the convention to begin with.

When you finally reach the front of the line and get to meet someone you admire, tell them. If a film or character has had an impact on you, let them know. Celebrities are people too. Everyone likes to hear nice things about themselves and the work they do. Depending on the size of the convention, you may have a minute or two to talk them.

...And Breathe

It is perfectly understandable why you would be excited when you meet a celebrity, but take a deep breath and be cool. You'll likely only have less than a minute to spend with them; don't waste it muttering "Oh my God! Oh my God! It's you." as you forget how to breathe and form coherent sentences. Most celebrities understand you may be nervous and will likely try to help you relax by asking you name or how you are doing.

Try to avoid going into full fan boy or girl meltdown. While it can be flattering to have someone freak out over you, it can also be a little awkward. Don't be nervous. Take a deep breath and introduce yourself.

Be Nice

When you meet them, be nice. Say hello. Ask how their day is going. Understand that just because they are at the convention, it doesn't mean they are having a good time. All it takes is one rude "fan" and they can start to have a bad day. Being polite and courteous will be far more appreciated. Telling them you didn't like their performance in a particular film or role or that you don't like their last painting, book or comic doesn't help anyone to have a good time.

If you don't appreciate a piece of their work, talk about a piece you do like. If you don't like the celebrity at all, save everyone some grief and move along. Being a smug halfwit makes you look like an ass and ruins it for everyone else. If you upset a guest, you've potentially ruined the event for the people behind you line if the guest is unable to shake the negativity

Shaking Hands

While shaking hands is nice, it is also the number one way that germs are spread around a convention. So bring some hand sanitizer. Some celebrities may be germophobes and won't shake hands. Don't take it personally. They don't want to take colds and flu back to their families as much you don't want to either.

AUTOGRAPHS

Most guests at events are there to meet fans, sign autographs and take photos. This is your opportunity to get up close and personal.

Autograph Prices

Shy of a few events, most conventions charge for celebrity autographs. Autograph prices at celebrity booths are not negotiable, so don't even try to talk them down. If they give you a discount, then they have to give everyone else a discount. Unless you are a close friend of one of the guests or they know you personally, there is no reason to offer a discount. They are there to make a living too. Asking for a break just makes everyone uncomfortable as the guests do not like telling people no. The argument of "I've paid for your career" doesn't fly, so don't even go there.

The prices are set by the celebrity. The convention generally has no control over how much a celebrity wants to charge. For standard guests and conventions you can usually expect to pay between $20 and $80 for an autograph. Some events may include the cost of the autograph in the ticket, but this is not typical. Research the event before you go, as most sites will post autograph prices beforehand so you can budget accordingly.

Consider an autograph to be an investment, even from the lesser name guests. Autographs tend to hold their value well and if the actor, actress, author or artist suddenly makes it big, the value of their autograph will increase significantly.

Not all celebrities will take credit cards, so be sure to have cash on hand, just in case.

No Inappropriate Comments.

When you finally get to the front of the line and get to approach the celebrity, do not drop a poster or photograph down in front of them and ask them to sign something crude or inappropriate. The only time this is acceptable is if the actor is famous for a crude or inappropriate character. Otherwise, don't step outside the boundaries of the actor's body of work.

A short dedication or a famous quote from their movies are the most appropriate requests. The majority of autographs I have collected have brief movie quotes on them such as "May the Force be with you" or "I'll be back".

Don't Abuse a Good Thing

Don't take advantage of their generosity. I was at a convention a while back and Robert Kirkman, the creator of the Walking Dead was a guest. All autographs were included with the ticket price. The guy in front of me drops a pile of at least one hundred and fifty comics down in front of him. The line backed up behind him and he started getting defensive when people started shouting at him. He was obviously nothing more than a scalper and abused the policies of the convention to make himself money. Don't be that person. The line will be eternally grateful. The policies changed the following year, but all it takes is one person to ruin it for everyone else.

PHOTO OPS

Photo ops are a wonderful way of capturing a memory with one of your favorite celebrities. While you can usually take a candid picture at their booths, many conventions will have a dedicated professional photo area where fans can take pictures.

Having your photo taken with a celebrity in the photo area is a great way to get creative and make the memory a fun one. The limits are only set up by the guest and your imagination. Make sure you are aware of their rules beforehand. Some will only want to be with you in the picture and not touching you. Some guests will hover hand you, while some will hug you and some are anything goes. Do some research online to see other pictures people may have posted to get a feel for how adventurous the celebrity is.

The Dreaded Lines

Celebrity signings and photo ops are two of the most common places you will see lines. Depending on the popularity of the celebrity, expect wait times to be hours long. Make sure the celebrity is worth the wait to you. You can easily lose half a day in line.

Seek Out Up-and-Coming Artists and Authors

Back in 2004, a struggling comic book artist was at San Diego Comicon trying to sell his new comic book about zombies. Fans weren't paying much attention and kept shuffling by like the zombies in his comic book. Little did they know that ten years later, Robert Kirkman would be one of the biggest names, not only in comic books, but also in television. First issues of The Walking Dead are now going for over five hundred times their original cover price.

You never know when the person struggling to sell the first edition of their comic book at a convention is going to be the next Stan Lee or Robert Kirkman. Everybody has to start somewhere. The artist's area is a great place to find the talent of tomorrow. You will find all kinds of pop culture and original artwork and comic books. Give them a chance to blow your mind.

PANELS

Most guests at an event will be involved in a panel at some point during the convention. Check with the event calendar to see when panels are scheduled. Panels are covered in greater depth in the next chapter.

One On One

Sometimes, if you are very lucky, you may get a one-on-one interaction with a celebrity. They could be walking the floor or waiting in a hallway. Always treat them exactly how you would expect to be treated, with respect and good manners. You (hopefully) wouldn't treat a stranger with disrespect, celebrities should be no different.

If you catch a guest off the clock and they are on the phone, please give them some privacy. They have families, wives, husbands and children they are away from when they are on the road.

If you happen to meet a celebrity on the convention floor and away from their booth, they are to be treated like any other attendee. Do not expect free autographs or photos. Some may be gracious enough to let you take a selfie with them, but it is not to be expected.

OFF THE CLOCK

Chances are good, that if you are staying at the same hotel the convention is using for the guests, you will run into one of them at the hotel bar. The same rules apply as when you meet them in their booth. Be polite and respectful when approaching them.

While they are technically off the clock, they are aware fans will recognize them and approach them. Don't suddenly scream out "OH MY GOD, STAN LEE IS SITTING AT THE BAR". This is a very bad idea because a) everyone in the bar will now know that Stan Lee is in there even if they didn't before and you will now have a much harder time to talking to him and b) Stan is likely to retreat to his room squashing any chance you would have had of an intimate one on one chat.

Some of my most amazing convention experiences have been meeting celebrities off the clock and having impromptu chats with them. If you are fortunate enough to find yourself in such an opportunity, make the most of it, chances are you may never get to do so again.

ATTENDING AS A GUEST

If you are attending a convention as a guest, make sure that your appearance agreement is in place prior to the start of the event. Never make assumptions that something is set in stone such as airfare, hotel or an appearance payment. While at the event, you should be focusing on meeting fans, taking photographs and signing autographs, not on contractual agreements.

CHAPTER TEN

PANELS

- **PANEL TYPES**
- **IN THE AUDIENCE**
- **THE RIGHT QUESTIONS**
- **TO HOST OR NOT TO HOST**

The main body of content of any convention is going to be focused around its programming. Programming consists of fan and guest panels focusing on particular elements of pop culture and fandom. These panels could be about costuming, movie trivia, con etiquette or franchise highlights, to name a few. Panels are either one speaker presenting on a topic or a group of people taking questions from the audience. Celebrity panels will likely be more of a fan Q&A session with a moderator acting as a buffer between the audience and guest.

Almost all attendees at convention panels will find themselves hosting panels, moderating panels or attending panels. Regardless of which side of paneling you are on, there are some basic rules to follow.

RECORDING

Before you head into a panel, be aware that most conventions do not allow panels or presentations to be recorded. These events are intended to be exclusive to attendees. If you are caught recording, you will likely be asked to leave the room and face the risk of possibly having your badge revoked.

PICK YOUR PANELS

As discussed earlier in the book, the chances of you being able to attend every panel or spotlight you want to are slim, especially at the larger conventions. As soon as the schedule is available, create a calendar of the events you would like to attend. If possible, try and find panels that are close to each other. If you attend a noon panel and hope to catch a 1:30 p.m. panel at the opposite end of the building, you may struggle to not only get there on time, but also to find a seat. Some events close the doors after the panel has started.

ASKING QUESTIONS

The whole point of Q&A sessions is for the audience to ask questions to whoever is on stage. Audience Q&A's are an amazing and possibly once in a lifetime opportunity to ask questions of some of your favorite celebrities and people you admire.

Before you throw yourself at the microphone, here are some tips to help get your question asked, the panelist gives an amazing answer and you get to sit back down as a hero.

No Self Promotion

Don't start with plugging your blog, podcast or website.

This is not about you and you will not get the response you are hoping for. The chances are very high that the celebrity on stage will not rush out to your Twitter page to follow you and most of the audience will forget almost instantly. There are plenty of times to network during the event. This is not one of them.

Keep It Brief

In order to keep the rest of the day's events running on schedule, there is only limited time for Q&A's. Be considerate to your fellow attendees and keep your question short. Don't ask a three part question and then keep adding on follow up questions. If fewer hands are popping up at the end, feel free to ask a second or even third, but let everyone have a turn before you ask more questions.

This Is Not About You

While this is an important moment for you, remember the question is about the guest on stage. No one is interested in your life story.

Starting with "I'm a huge fan" is okay, but going off on a tangent about how they have influenced your poetry and you've followed their every move on Twitter and Facebook and named seven of your cats after their lead characters is tedious for the audience and can get a little creepy for the panelist.

Everyone understands that this could be an important moment for you, but try not to lose focus.

You Do Have a Question, Don't You?

This is not an opportunity for you to ramble on for two minutes about how much you liked them in a particular movie and how you related to the character. Remember, it is a question and answer event, not a statement event.

Keep It Classy

There is nothing worse than an audience member asking a rude or offensive question of the person on stage. I've been in the audience when someone has done it and I've been on stage when someone has asked me a deliberately offensive question and quite frankly, it sucks. You can feel the fun and joy being sucked out of the room. You may get a giggle from the one or two people in your group, but for the rest of the audience, it is extremely uncomfortable.

It is okay to be clever or witty, but make sure you cut to the chase and ask something really good or don't waste everyone's time. It helps to bounce your question off the new friends you made in line. Remember, when you ask a question of a celebrity or panelist, you represent other fans. Don't make us look like jerks.

This isn't to say that questions can't be personal or controversial. Some of the best responses I've heard have been to personal, but sincere questions.

Don't Get Too Personal

Don't dig for dirt. Most professionals on stage will not insult other professionals unless it is done in jest or firmly tongue-in-cheek. It is not good for a person's career to start tearing down others when they get on a soapbox.

How much money a person made on a particular movie or project is none of your business. You wouldn't ask a coworker or your boss how much they make, this should be no different. Similarly, do not ask about sensitive questions related to legal matters such as divorce, child custody issues or other criminal infractions. Remember, what you see in the press is only half the story. Many times it is sensationalized and elements are exaggerated if not altogether false. You are all here for a good time. Bringing up a messy divorce is the fastest way to suck the positive energy out of the room.

Do ask:

"What made you decide on taking the role in __ "
"Which was your favorite project?"
"Who do you enjoy working with the most?"
"If you could be in any other profession, which would it be?"

Do not ask:

"How does it feel that most of your costars from __ are dead?
"If you could punch any costar in the face, who would it be?"
"Who have you slept with in Hollywood?"
"Do you regret marrying __?"

Dirt, while initially entertaining, is not good business for celebrities. How would you feel if a coworker took to public forums announcing that they wanted to punch you in the face or couldn't stand working with you? It wouldn't make for a particularly fun work environment. Certainly there are celebrities who enjoy dishing dirt either in a sincere or tongue-in-cheek manner, but let that flow organically if it is going to come out. There are some celebrities who do like controversy. Fishing for dirt just puts everyone on the defense and it makes for an uncomfortable panel that both guests and audiences can't wait to get away from.

Be Careful With the Minutia

The questions that deal with the heavy minutia of a franchise are frequently not known to the celebrities who were involved. While you may be dying to know which brand of hydro spanner Han Solo used to fix the Millennium Falcon in The Empire Strikes Back, chances are Harrison Ford doesn't know. Depending on the actor, they may not even care. The truth is most actors and actresses have moved on to other roles. It is a lot easier for fans to stay in the franchise than the actors involved.

If you ask this type of question, you are probably going to get glossed over very quickly. This doesn't make your question any less important to you; just realize there are better places to find this kind of answer. We have this wonderful tool called the internet. Due to the wealth of literature based around Han Solo, it would be impossible for Harrison Ford to know every element of the character's backstory. Don't get upset if the actor can't give an answer on the exact course he took during the Kessel Run.

The whole point of the Q&A session is to have fun and hear some wonderful stories or anecdotes, it is not to embarrass or stump the guests.

WHAT IF I SEE EXCLUSIVE VIDEO FOOTAGE?

Some of the bigger conventions will show exclusive footage to a much hyped television show or movie. Consider yourself lucky that you have been included with a select few to be able to see something the rest of the world may not see for many months down the road. Do not, under any circumstances whip out your cell phone and take low quality footage to share on Facebook or YouTube. You may face legal action if you're caught.

ATTENDING A FAN PANEL

Many panels are hosted by fans and they are there to share their love of fandom with the audience. The same rules apply. Just because the panelist isn't famous, it doesn't mean that they haven't earned the right to get respect from the audience.

Remember, everyone is human and we make all mistakes. If someone on the panel gets something wrong, there is a right way and a wrong way to handle it. For example:

Panelist: "Tom Baker, the fifth Doctor..."

Immediately alarms go off in your head. Do you:

a) Leap out of your seat yelling "Tom Baker wasn't the fifth doctor! He was the fourth. Peter Davison was the fifth. You are a fraud and a liar!"
b) Laugh under your breath, but loud enough for everyone to hear you and know your disapproval.
c) Let it go. We're all human and we all make mistakes. A mistake does not equate lack of knowledge on a subject. More than likely it is just good old fashioned nerves.

Sure, you *can* chose *a* or *b*, but most people will think you're an ass and the presenter will get flustered. Trust me, I know, I've had it done to me. Everyone makes mistakes, even the panelists on stage. Some may not be used to be speaking to large crowds or they may have a lot going on their head trying to keep the panel on track. At a recent convention, I was hosting a zombie panel and immediately went to host a Star Wars panel. During the second presentation, I called George Lucas (the guy famous for Star Wars) George Romero (the guy famous for zombies). Immediately a hand shoots up "Dude, George Romero didn't direct Star Wars. Do you even know what you're talking about?" Yes, I knew what I was talking about.

Mistakes happen. Roll with it and just let it go. Don't immediately shout out to correct them. If you feel the need to correct them, politely talk to them after the panel and address your comment as a question.

If letting it go just isn't in your nature and you have to say something, at least word it nicely.

"Hey, I was wondering which Star Wars movie Romero directed, as I've only seen his zombie work". This light hearted question stops any tension that could have formed and immediately lightens the mood.

GETTING INTO A PANEL

Depending on the popularity of the topic of the panel and the guest hosting it, lines can form hours before the panel begins. Many of the more popular panels are full before the doors even open.

Some events clear the room from the previous panel, however many do not due to time restrictions and keeping things on schedule. If there is a panel you are dying to get into, consider going to the previous panel in that room and sitting through it to guarantee yourself a spot at the panel you want to attend.

HOSTING A PANEL

Many conventions allow for fans and guests to submit applications to host a panel or presentation. Hosting either a solo or group panel can be very rewarding experience; however, there is a lot of work involved in getting it put together.

Most conventions will compensate your time with a free ticket for the day you are presenting in exchange for your expertise, but consider the trade off before committing to it. You will spend many hours preparing for your presentation between creating slides and practicing. If you do not practice, the audience will notice. I calculate I spend on average twelve hours preparing per hour long panel I present. Make sure that the tradeoff is worth it to you. It is a considerable investment of your time

Should I Host a Panel?'

That is a question only you can answer. To see if you should, ask yourself these questions.

1) Is there a topic you consider yourself to be an authority or expert on?
2) Can you present your knowledge in a format that is interesting to the audience?
3) Are you comfortable speaking in front of a room full of people? How about a room only at 5% capacity?

When you are on the stage, the audience looks to you to be the professional. Not just in how you present yourself, but on your knowledge of the subject at hand. You are the expert and fans attending your panel will expect you to know as much, if not more than they do. If the audience feels they know more about the topic, you will lose their interest fast. However, on the opposite side of that, if you have an hour of material they have never heard before or are unable to relate to, you may still lose their interest. The trick is to find the balance between sharing popular knowledge so the audience can relate and reeling them in with new information.

Do Not Be a No-Show

If you have signed yourself up to run a panel or solo presentation, you have a responsibility to follow through with your commitment. Remember there are attendees who are counting on you to prepare and be ready to present and most of all show up for your panel. Some attendees may have moved plans around or missed another panel to be at yours. It is understood that you are volunteering your time and while that is admirable, simply not showing up is not only rude, but very disrespectful. You will likely not be invited back to present at a future event.

Convention organizers understand that sometimes life can get in the way, but a courtesy phone call to say you can't make it goes a long way. However, have a valid reason. Don't cancel because you can't be bothered or over slept. Convention programming is built around volunteers. If everyone decided to not show up, the convention would have a lot of upset attendees.

If you sign up, show up.

EQUIPMENT

Before you arrive at the convention center or venue, determine your IT needs in order to successfully be able to present to the audience. Generally this includes:

- Microphone (handheld or lavaliere)
- Laptop
- Projector
- Internet connection

Keep in mind that not every convention center or venue will have the latest and greatest presentation equipment available. Do not assume that they will have everything you need. Check with the event coordinators to find out what equipment is available to you. You may need to bring your own laptop or you may have to run without any equipment at all.

Don't spend weeks preparing a presentation only to get to the venue and find out that they do not have any equipment available. It does happen. The event usually has to rent the equipment from the venue, so rental cost may be a factor.

CREATING A PRESENTATION

PowerPoint can be as much your enemy as it can be your friend if you do not use it correctly. Presenters walk a fine line between showing a PowerPoint slide show that is informative and well designed and a presentation that is a distraction and actually pulls the audience way from the information being delivered.

Do not create slides full of nothing but text. The slides are there to serve as bullet points and not as a script. The audience does not want to see you reading your script from the slides. You should know the content well enough to be able to use your presentation with just the bullet points. The slides are designed to keep the panel on track. If an audience can simply read your presentation, why do they need you there?

Make sure that your font and background colors complement each other. Do not choose a font color that can get lost in the background.

Do not use small or hard to read fonts. Sure, your presentation may look fancy, but if the audience is struggling to read the fancy cursive cartoon font you are using, they will lose interest fast.

Do not use excessive audio and video. Transition or audio effects may look and sound cute when you are rehearsing, but they can get distracting very quickly and can draw attention away from the content of your slides.

Engage Your Audience

While this is your panel, the audience is just as important.

Keep them engaged. The quickest way to combat nerves is to ask a question. You should value the audience's input as much as they value yours. Before long it is like chatting with old friends.

If you don't know the answer to a question, it is perfectly okay to say you don't know. However, instead of just saying "I don't know" and glossing over the question, use it as a tool to generate a discussion with the audience. A great conversation can come from a question you don't the answer to. The whole purpose of panels is to share passion and knowledge. No one knows everything.

The Audience Is On Your Side

The audience wants you to succeed, they really do. They don't want to see you make mistakes, lose your train of thought or make a fool of yourself. They want to have fun. They are on your side and will stick with you until the end of the panel. If you lose your place, take a breath and pause.

STORAGE

Most venues will not provide storage for props or additional items you may need for your presentation. You will need to arrange to drop them off and pick them up immediately before and after your panel.

MODERATORS

The role of a moderator is to ensure a panel runs successfully. A moderator introduces the speaker and acts a buffer between the guest and the audience. Depending on the venue and available staff, you may or may not have a moderator on hand. Be prepared either way. If you do have a moderator, prepare a brief bio so they can introduce you to the audience.

CHAPTER ELEVEN

CREEPERS, BULLIES & SEXUAL HARASSMENT

- ● THE DEFINITION OF HARASSMENT
- ● PROTECT YOURSELF
- ● RESPECT EVERYONE
- ● DON'T FEAR THE CREEPER

*I*t is time to put on the serious hat for this chapter. While I have spent most of this book writing about all of the fun to be had at an event, in recent years, a dark cloud has been cast over the convention circuit that has drawn attention from international media outlets. I am talking about sexual and non-sexual harassment.

It unfortunate and saddening that there needs to be a section that discusses on the darker side of conventions in a book that is highlighting the fun and excitement of attending.

However, sexual harassment and bullying are very real issues affecting attendees and to ignore them would be a huge disservice to the people who sadly have had to deal with this type of behavior at events.

Convention harassment has been receiving a lot of press coverage in recent months. There have been stories of abuse, both sexual and non-sexual harassment, bullying, assault and even rape. Yes, at conventions. At comicons. It is abhorrent. What has happened? This never used to be the case. Things have changed and it is important we get things back on track.

While more and more conventions are taking a stand on this kind of behavior, there is still a long way to go to completely remove this dark mark from the convention circuit. Many events are including harassment policies on their websites and are punishing offenders.

HARASSMENT

Harassment is defined as disruptive and intimidating behavior that includes offensive comments based on an attendee's gender, age, race, sexual orientation, disability, physical appearance or religion. It also includes bullying, inappropriate sexual or non-sexual contact, physical or cyber stalking during and after the event, and harassing photography. Be conscious of your actions, you may be harassing someone and do not even realize it.

BE AWARE

The goal of this chapter is not to dissuade you from going to an event. Quite the opposite, in fact. This chapter is designed to help you deal with troublesome attendees so you can get on and enjoy the event. No one should ever feel they have to be harassed by another attendee. This group of attendees is in the minority, but they do exist and you should be ready.

Earlier in the book I discuss conventions going mainstream. While going mainstream has helped conventions grow, it has brought its own set of problems. Opening the doors to a wider market allows people from all walks of life to enter. With the rapid growth in popularity, it is no longer a small social clique of comic book collectors who attend the events. As the popularity grows, the number of attendees grows and yes, this sadly means that there will be a handful of unsavory characters at events.

RESPECT

This has been mentioned before, but it warrants repeating. The key thing to remember is to have respect for your fellow convention attendees. Whether they are male, female, young, old, fully clothed, skimpily dressed, cosplaying well, cosplaying poorly, treat *EVERYONE* with respect. A convention is not a meat market or open dating pool. If you want that kind of environment, there are plenty of night clubs out there that can cater to that need. Conventions are a safe zone. Women or men in revealing costumes are not there to be ridiculed, harassed or embarrassed. They are there to have fun.

If at any time you are accosted, sexually assaulted or feel threatened, call the police. Do not just flag down an event staff member, as many times they are volunteers and are not trained to deal with physical confrontations. Call 9-1-1. If you were accosted at a grocery store you would do the same thing. Don't let the fact that you are at a convention and in a costume deter you from having the right to protect yourself.

WHAT IS A CREEPER?

A creeper is someone whose behavior is inappropriate and

quite frankly creeps people out. This behavior could include taking intentionally indecent photographs or asking sexual questions in a panel. This is the person who gets a little too close in a photo op or has a mirror on their shoe to see up women's skirts. Yes, sadly these people exist.

SEXY DOES NOT EQUATE CONSENT

The young lady dressed up as Princess Leia in her slave bikini? She feels strong and empowered. This does not make her a slut or easy, any more than a woman on the beach in a bikini is up for grabs. Just because a person is dressed sexy or revealing, it does not mean they are prowling the convention floor looking for a date. Besides, even if they are single, the chances of getting their attention through groping or crude comments are slim to non-existent.

If you are taking a photograph with a costumer, do not suddenly get a case of wandering hands. Butts, breasts and other private areas are 100% percent, absolutely, positively off limits. No ifs ands or buts about it. Don't be surprised if you get slapped, pushed or punched for doing so.

This is not just limited to women. A skimpy or revealing costume worn by either a man or a woman is not an open invitation to feel them up. The costumer's gender does not matter. A man dressed up as He-Man or Khal Drogo from Game of Thrones is as off limits as a female dressed up as Wonder Woman. You will find few costumers male or female who enjoy being felt up by strangers.

At no time ever, is it ever okay to grope, touch, feel or molest them in any way. That includes men groping women, women groping men, men groping men and women groping women. Respect people's boundaries. Even though someone is dressed up in revealing clothing, it does not make them a slut, whore or an easy target. They are not walking around waiting for someone to grab their ass or whistle.

WATCH YOUR MOUTH

In addition to the wandering hands, make sure you watch your tongue and what comes out of your mouth as well. Making crass and rude comments not only makes you look like a fool, but it makes those around you uncomfortable. No one finds it entertaining to hear sexual comments about a costumer.

As a parent to a little girl who looks up to Wonder Woman, I don't want to have to explain to her why someone is saying bad words to her favorite character or Wonder Woman's reaction to said comments. Remember, most conventions are family events, there are kids present and they look up to these characters. If you can't show restraint for a few hours, maybe it is best you stay home.

TRUST YOUR GUT

If someone taking a picture with you is making you feel uncomfortable, you do not have to put up with it. You are fully in control of the situation. If a hand wanders while you are posing, you do not even owe them the courtesy of a warning. You walk away. They had one chance to be decent and they blew it. You do not owe them a picture or any more of your time. If they can't treat you with respect, they aren't deserving of your time.

SUPPORT

In chapter eight, I discuss bringing a costume wrangler to an event to help navigate the crowds. You don't have to be wearing a large costume with blind spots to warrant a wrangler. A wrangler can also act as a buffer for overzealous fans wanting pictures. They can help keep lines moving and run interference if someone is getting out of hand.

IF YOU HEAR SOMETHING, SAY SOMETHING

Most people make crude public comments to other attendees just to get attention. They make these comments to get laughter. If you hear someone making rude comments about a costumer or cosplayer, say something. Let them know it isn't cool to talk crap about other attendees.

SOME CON-TACT

While walking around the convention, you will see all kinds of people in all kinds of costumes. Some of the costumes you will love, while others you may not. Making rude comments about how people look isn't funny or entertaining. Calling people out by their physical appearance is nothing more than bullying. Conventions are safe places for people to hang out and be who they are. Free of criticism and judgment.

Always remember, there is a person under the mask and makeup. Comicon allows for everyone attending to express themselves. You may not agree with the costume choices a particular person has made, but it is best if you keep these opinions to yourself. Not every man is 6'4" and ripped like a body builder. Just as not every woman is a 5'10" sized 2. Not everyone is going to look exactly like the source material. I've seen an overweight Spiderman, I've seen an Incredible Hulk who could not have been have more than 5'4" and 140lbs soaking wet. I've seen a seventy year old Supergirl. I have a seen a five foot Superman in screen accurate costume. Many of them I am lucky enough to call friends.

There is nothing written anywhere to say that an attendee in costume has to be screen accurate, not only in costume, but in build and in height. If that were the case, we'd see very few cosplayers at conventions, as so few would be able to cosplay the characters they like, myself included. After all, I am a little tall for a Stormtrooper. These people do not deserve to be mocked or laughed at, they should be praised for their confidence in being comfortable enough to throw off the shrouds of social stigma and labels and being comfortable with their fandom. People are generally very aware of their self-image and don't need someone shouting from the crowd that it looks like they just ate Captain America. If you can do better, step out of the peanut gallery and join in. Else just zip it.

People should never go to a convention and be made to feel bad about themselves. Yes, everyone does need to get along. This isn't a tree-hugging "be nice to everyone" comment. It is a "respect everyone" comment. Conventions are safe zones where people can be themselves. The whole concept of a convention is fans gathering to celebrate mutual adoration for a franchise or genre. If you think you're better than the attendees and talk down to them, attendees don't want you there as much as you don't want to be there. Do everyone a favor and stay home.

MEME'S

In recent years, memes have become a popular fad on the internet. A meme is usually a photograph with a line or two of text beneath it addressing the person in the picture. In many cases the comment is insulting to the victim. Yes, the person is a victim.

What many people fail to remember is that the person in the photo is a real person. No one wants to be the butt of people's jokes. Under no circumstances never, **EVER** take photographs of attendees and upload them to Facebook as a meme mocking them. It is a completely crap thing to do.

I'm active in a number of social circles and have on more

than one occasion seen a meme circulate with a friend's photo attached. It sucks when you can put a real life face to the image. Some were able to shrug it off, but others most certainly were not.

BULLYING

Costumers do not suddenly become bullet proof when they put on armor. Words hurt just as much whether you are Iron Man or a timid geek. If you see someone whose costume may not be the most flattering, it is best to keep your opinions to yourself.

Suicide

Bullying isn't just about making fun of someone in their costume, having a laugh and heading home. There are serious repercussions that go along with bullying.

There are numerous studies that link bullying to suicide. According to the Center for Disease Control, suicide is the third leading cause of death among young people, resulting in about 4,400 deaths per year. For every suicide among young people, there are at least one hundred attempts. These are very scary numbers.

Victims of bullying are between two to nine times more likely to consider suicide than non-victims. Think about that before posting an image online mocking an innocent attendee who did nothing to you.

Cyber Bullying

Cyber bullying is one of the leading causes of teenage death in the US and the circulation of meme's and harassment does little more than add fuel to the fire. With the speed information and misinformation travels online, the chances of the image getting back to the victim are high and once something is on the internet, it never goes away. That is a harsh reality that more and more people are discovering on an all too frequent basis.

Costumers are what make a convention so enjoyable. I could spend hours just people watching and taking in all of the amazing costumes and not once have I ever made a negative or snide comment about someone's appearance. Comicon is a time to escape bullying and teasing. It is a safe place for everyone involved.

INTERVIEWS GONE BAD

Recently, there have been reports of attendees acquiring media or press passes to conduct interviews for their website. Instead of asking legitimate questions related to the cosplayer or their costume, they are using their credentials to interview and harass female attendees with sexually charged questions and unwanted physical contact. While I will not address the guilty parties by name, their disgraceful actions deserve attention as they are casting an even darker shadow over the convention circuit and they should be ashamed of themselves.

Be aware that this type of behavior is occurring. If you are ever interviewed at a convention and the interviewer starts asking highly personal or sexual questions or behaves inappropriately, politely but firmly tell them the interview is over and leave. You are under no obligation to put up with disrespectful behavior.

Make sure you get the person's name and website details so you can report them to the event coordinators. It is important they do not gain access to media passes at future events.

CHAPTER TWELVE

SAFETY

- **PERSONAL SAFETY**
- **AFTER PARTY AWARENESS**
- **PROTECTING YOURSELF**
- **GETTING HOME SAFELY**

*J*ust because the main convention hall has closed for the day, it doesn't mean the event is over. The after-con nightlife is likely now only just getting started.

Many of the larger conventions have a considerable amount of after-parties and events geared towards adults attendees. This chapter will help you to navigate these events and get you home at the end of the evening.   Arriving home safely after the event has finished is just as important as staying safe during the day.

PROTECTING YOURSELF

The shameful acts of a few, mean there are steps that should be taken to keep you safe. While there are certainly cases of men being harassed, the reality is that women are far more frequently the victims. Many of the following steps, while appropriate for conventions can also be applied to keeping safe in everyday life.

Stay in open and pubic areas with your badge on display at all times.

Establish a firm line for what you consider appropriate and inappropriate behavior and stick to it. Do not allow strangers to cross those boundaries.

If you are harassed, report it. Do not just ignore the behavior. Event security will likely remove the suspect from the convention hall or after-party venue.

Be careful who you share your personal contact information with. There are many unfortunate tales of stalking that have started at a convention and followed into everyday life.

AFTER PARTIES

The after parties are a lot of fun, but can be a prime place for the behavior found at nightclubs. To prevent yourself from becoming a victim, use the following steps to help minimize your chances of harassment.

If you are drinking alcohol, drink clear drinks. When you are done drinking, you can easily switch to 7-Up or Sprite with a twist of lime and continue having a good time. People will think you are still drinking and most likely won't offer you another. It is also easier to see if a clear drink has been tampered with.

Keep your drink with you at all times. Drinks can and do get drugged. Having a drink spiked does not just mean date-rape drugs; someone can just as easily order you a drink with two or three shots without telling you. Do not accept a drink from a stranger unless you watched the drink being poured. If it doubt, dump it out.

If you start to feel strange, such as dizzy, light headed, sick or confused, find a friend and tell them to get you out of the event and somewhere safe. You need medical attention.

Always have a designated driver. This one goes without saying. Never drink and drive.

Always have a wing man. Two brains and sets of eyes are always better than one.

If you meet someone at an event or party, take a moment to snap their picture and send it to a friend or family member. If you are in the picture, that is even better. If their intentions are honorable, they won't mind. If they have bad motives, they will make themselves scarce as they won't want their picture used as evidence.

Always let people know where you are, what you're doing, who you are doing it with and where you are going next. This isn't so people can check up on you, this is a CYA (cover your ass) in case things do go bad. If a less than scrupulous person picks you up at an after party and no one knows where you are, you'll have no back up.

If you are bringing a minor to the event, you are their guardian. You are responsible for their well-being. Do not let them leave with a different group and do not give them alcohol or illegal substances.

LEAVING THE EVENT

Event organizers want you to get home safely after an event

or after party. As with chapter eleven, the tips in this chapter are not to dissuade you from going to an event. They are to keep you aware of security risks and how to alleviate them.

Always make sure you carry a cell phone with you in case of emergencies. Your cell phone can very quickly become a lifesaving tool. Make sure it is charged before you leave the event, as a dead cell phone is about as much use as a bar of chocolate.

There is always safety in numbers. If you can leave an event with a group, your chances of running into sinister characters decrease significantly.

Always be aware of your surroundings.

Walking

Many conventions are held in city centers and many city centers have dark alleyways and shady areas. Do not walk alone in an alley, or drive in a bad neighborhood at night. There are even some should even be avoided during the day.

Always walk with confidence. Keep your head up, swing your arms and don't slouch. Confidence scares off a lot of people who are looking expressly for victims who won't put up a fight.

When walking on sidewalks, always try to walk facing on-coming traffic to avoid curb crawlers. Wherever possible stay on a sidewalk with street lights.

If a vehicle does pull up beside you, turn and walk in the opposite direction. On the opposite side of that, if you are driving and simply need directions, go to a gas station. Do not stop a lone pedestrian on the street. You are likely to get ignored or maced.

If you have reason think you are being followed, cross the street. If they turn around, cross the street again. Try to find a busy area and head there.

If you ever find yourself in danger, your voice is your best weapon. Shouting, 'Call the police' will get people's attentions very quickly and the potential assailant will make themselves scarce.

Car Safety

Always try and park your car under a street lamp or well-lit area wherever possible. Also, if you can, park on the front end of an aisle so your back is not to another car.

If you find yourself parked next to a van, enter your car from the passenger door. Most abductors attack their victims by grabbing them and pulling them into their vehicle while a victim's back is turned. If there is a car parked next to the driver's side of your car, look in the window. If you see a single passenger sitting alone in the seat nearest your car, you may want to walk back into the venue and get event security. If you are concerned, ask security to walk you to your car. It is their job to keep you safe.

If you have parked in a parking garage, always use an elevator instead of a stairwell to get to your floor. If you are not comfortable getting in an elevator with someone in there, wait for the next one. If someone gets on at a floor and makes you uncomfortable, get off on the next floor.

Always have your keys ready before approaching your car and check the back seat and passenger floor before getting in.

Once you get into your car, don't loiter. Lock the doors, start the engine, put on your seatbelt and leave. If you are distracted with a phone or tuning the stereo, your attention is not on your surroundings.

Taxi Cabs

Do not hail a minicab from the street or accept a lift from a minicab looking for potential customers. You have no way of knowing if the driver is a legitimate cab driver. Always book a cab over the phone and when the cab arrives, verify what name of the client they are expecting to pick up. Make sure your cell phone has the number of a few reputable taxi companies in your contact list.

Whenever possible, try to share a cab ride with at least one other friend. Always sit in the back of a cab and if you get chatting to the driver, do not give away personal details such as who you live with or what is waiting for you at the end of the trip.

Public Transport

Always wait for a bus or train in a well-lit area near to other people wherever possible and have your ticket, pass or change ready in your hand so that your wallet or purse is out of sight.

Avoid empty carriages or carriages with one passenger. Try to sit in areas where there are lots of other people. If you feel uncomfortable, move to another seat or carriage.

If a bus is empty or it is after dark, stay as near as possible to the driver. Most buses are equipped with cameras. If you feel threatened make as much noise as possible to attract the attention of the driver or guard.

Most importantly, trust your instincts. If something doesn't feel right, it probably isn't.

PART III

AFTER THE EVENT

CHAPTER THIRTEEN

POST-CONVENTION

- **REST UP**
- **SURVEY SAYS**
- **FOLLOWING UP**
- **PLANNING THE NEXT EVENT**

*S*orry to be the bearer of bad news, but at some point it is inevitable that the convention will eventually draw to a close. The guests will go home, the vendors will pack up their wares and the next day, the panel rooms will be full of business meetings and seminars with not a costumed person in sight.

Once the event is over, it is time to head back to normal everyday life. Some go back to their non-con lives, but a dedicated few immediately start planning for the next convention. It could be the same event a year from now or a completely different convention a month later. The great thing about conventions is that no matter where you live, there is always another just around the corner.

However, before you start planning your next convention excursion, you'll most likely have some housekeeping items from this event to take care of first.

CON HANGOVER AND CON CRUD

You've been on your feet for the good part of two, three or maybe even four days and you've probably not slept enough. Spend some time decompressing so you don't get sick. You've likely been around sick people and your immune system is quite possibly hanging on by a thread.

Sleeping a few hours a night during the convention is fine, but it will catch up with you. If you have to drive back home, make sure you are rested before you take on a long road trip.

SURVEYS

Whatever your next move is going to be, an after event review is always worth considering. Communication will not only help you, but every other attendee at the next convention.

The only way a convention can continue to grow and improve is if people speak up. Many conventions will send out questionnaires or surveys to attendees so they can determine what worked and what did not. Use this opportunity to let them know about your experience. Don't just dwell on the negative issues; they also need to know what you enjoyed. Tell them what you liked about the event and which guests you enjoyed meeting.

Keep in mind that there is only so much a convention can do to make an event better. If no one reports elements that need to be fixed, nothing will change. The surveys are sent out for a reason, to solicit feedback. Instead of taking to the internet to complain about the event, use the channels the event organizers provide to offer constructive feedback.

What Worked and What Didn't

Remember that not every issue you experience at a convention is the fault of the venue or event planners. Sometime things just don't work out. Make note of what did and did not work for you. If you missed out on getting a particular exclusive, try to figure out why. Did you not get there fast enough and were distracted by other vendors? Did you park at the wrong of the venue or did they simply just sell out in a few minutes? Did you miss a panel because of mismanaging time? Giving the event a replay in your mind can help alleviate the same issues the next time you go.

MAKING CONNECTIONS

Throughout the event, you will likely receive business cards from various attendees, either on a personal level or as business acquaintants. Be sure to reach out to them in a timely manner. If you have been hosting a panel, contacting them six months later after they have forgotten your panel is not the best way to get them to remember you. They will have likely long forgotten who you are. Communication is key to successful networking.

Facebook Invites

You will have no doubt met and exchanged information with many new people and many will simply say "track me down on Facebook". You are also likely to receive a fair number of Facebook invites in return. Remember Facebook can get a little snotty with too many friend invites. If too many people reject your invites, you can get blocked from adding new friends. Not that I would know anything about that.

Also, be aware that if you send someone you don't know a message, it goes into their *Other* folder and they do not get notification that you messaged them and it just sits there until they look in the folder. However, you can pay Facebook $.99 to send the message directly to their inbox for you.

When networking at an event, always mention who you are on Facebook and that you will reach out after the event is over. That way they are expecting your invite and hopefully won't flag you as spam when they receive it.

Building your network can get you invites to other events and broaden your convention scope.

UPLOADING PICTURES

Don't forget to upload all of the pictures you have taken over the weekend and share them on your various online profiles. Everyone loves seeing all of the wonderful sights of a convention. It may even spur people into attending a future event themselves.

FUTURE EVENTS

Keep an eye out on social media tools for other events happening in your area. You may be surprised at how many conventions are going on just in your city alone. It is a busy market and getting busier by the month.

See you at the next convention!

22454988R00066

Made in the USA
San Bernardino, CA
06 July 2015